GW00750928

THE LAUGHING CRICKETER OF WOMBWELL

THE LAUGHING CRICKETER OF WOMBWELL

by
Mick Pope

Darf Publishers
London

First published 1990
by Darf Publishers Ltd

ISBN 1 85077 219 3 (Hard cased)
ISBN 1 85077 224 X (Paperback)

Printed in Great Britain by BPCC Wheatons Ltd., Exeter
Cover by Sue Sharples

This book is dedicated to the memory
of my Father
Charles Edwin Pope (1911-1986)

CONTENTS

LIST OF ILLUSTRATIONS

ACKNOWLEDGEMENTS

Many people have assisted during the production of this book and in particular the author would like to thank the following:

Sir Donald Bradman for kindly allowing me to use his tribute to Roy Kilner as the foreword to this book.

Thanks also to Jack Sokell for his constant help and encouragement and for writing the introduction.

Michelle Routledge who has read through the entire book during its various stages.

I would also like to thank in particular Tony Woodhouse for allowing me to reproduce many photographs from his collection and for his assistance in various other ways.

Roy Wilkinson also deserves special mention for without his expert statistical contribution this biography would be incomplete.

Grateful thanks also to the following for their assistance and help:

Barnsley Central Library, A. Bradley, K.A. Bradley, Rob Brooke, Irving Fairhust, Keith Farnsworth, David Frith, Mr G.L. Greaves, Mrs M. Kilner, Leeds Central Library, David Mangham, Ian Rigby, Sheffield Central Library, The Star, Ken Sykes, Mrs Taylor, Ken Utley, Jack Varney, Peter Wynne-Thomas and The Yorkshire Post.

FOREWORD

In recalling a former colleague or adversary there is usually a tinge of sadness about his passing, especially if it is premature and a prospective brilliant career has been cut down in the flower of its youth.

One such was the case of my chum Archie Jackson, the legendary young Australian batsman whose vast potential was terminated when he was a mere 23.

I can't quite say the same about Roy Kilner. But I can say he died much too young and at an age when his cricket prowess had not quite run its expected course.

Roy represented England at home against Australia and South Africa. Against Australia in Australia in 1924–5, his part in England's win in the 4th Test at Melbourne is still memorable. As a bowler his figures in the 5 Tests were second only to those of the great Maurice Tate, the latter's form in that season being regarded as the pinnacle of his career.

I knew of Roy by reputation only but we had an oblique association. When I was a youth my mother had promised to buy me a cricket bat if I made a century in a certain country game and I duly won this coveted prize – my first new bat ever.

I visited a sports store and selected a Roy Kilner bat. To this day I recall the unusual branding which began and ended with a large R – to wit Roy KilneR, and I promptly called it the Rolls Royce of cricket bats – the big R.R. which adorned the Rolls Royce motor cars being well known to me.

The bat was made by Wm Sykes Ltd of Horbury, Yorkshire, and years later, when my own name appeared on cricket bats, I, too, chose as my manufacturer Wm Sykes Ltd, and I henceforth used 'Sykes' bats throughout my career.

On my first tour of England in 1930 it is probable that I would have played against Roy had not a fatal infection ended his life a year or two before our arrival. But as a tribute to his memory the Australian team members visited his grave and laid a wreath on it as a mark of respect. We would have preferred his company on the square he loved so much.

As a player he undoubtedly embraced the typical Yorkshire qualities of

The 1930 Australian Tourists pay their respects to the late Roy Kilner during their visit to Wombwell. The young genius batsman Don Bradman is pictured on the front row, second from the left amongst those in the light coloured suits. (By kind permission of Irving Fairhurst.)

dourness and doggedness but as a man he was revered for his charm, humour and generosity.

To this day I believe I am the only foreigner to be honoured with Life Membership of the Yorkshire County Cricket club so I belatedly share a companionship with one whose life enriched his club and formed part of its imperishable tradition.

I join with the thousands of others who salute his memory.

SIR DONALD BRADMAN, A.C.,
Adelaide,
February 1989.

INTRODUCTION

When Tony Woodhouse, Roy Wilkinson and myself wrote *Cricketers of Wombwell* we had the advantage of being able to spend much time with Norman Kilner and other members of the Kilner family and we also received valuable help from Arthur Gilligan and Leslie Deakins.

Mick Pope has not been able to have such help with this book on Roy Kilner due to the demise of Norman and Arthur but, undaunted, he has delved and researched far and wide in this obvious 'labour of love' on a very special cricketer and the result deserves to be a best-seller.

Roy must have been very special when one realises that he had a huge benefit of over £4,000 in 1925 which was a record until 1945. Equally amazing is the fact that over 100,000 people crowded the small mining village of Wombwell for his funeral in 1928. These were days when few people had motor cars but such was the love for this happiest of players that many people walked several miles to pay their tribute. Two years later the Australian team visited his grave and 60 years on it is a lasting tribute to think that Sir Donald Bradman recalls the visit.

One may ask "How would Roy have fared in modern cricket?" – He would undoubtably still have captured people's imaginations by his endeavours to entertain and would certainly have continued to remain happy and contented.

When *Cricketers of Wombwell* was written, Wombwell Cricket Lovers Society was in its infancy but now it is playing its part in encouraging a love of cricket and especially encouraging local youngsters to enjoy the game. The Society feels proud that locals such as Martyn Moxon, Arnie Sidebottom, Tim Boon and Darren Gough have blossomed from our coaching classes and that in 1990 Wombwell is playing a part in Yorkshire cricket as it did in the days of Roy Kilner.

Our Society's weekly speaker meetings are always happy occasions and I feel that the happy spirit of Roy is still around to help us realise that cricket is a game to love and cherish despite the modern 'problems' associated with Yorkshire cricket and elsewhere.

The author, to his credit, has unearthed many new facts of Roy's life and career and this should please those who saw him play, those who cherish his memory and hopefully rekindle in the hearts of younger people, the joy and delight that Roy gave to many people.

Fittingly this book arrives in 1990, the centenary of Roy's birth, a year that will see special events in his native Wombwell as they remember with pride Roy and all he achieved.

Roy died too young and this in turn affected the progression and future of Yorkshire's heritage of left arm slow bowlers. If he had survived, it could have meant a delay in the emergence of Hedley Verity. Who knows? These are questions which will go unanswered.

I wish Mick Pope success with this, his first book, and grateful that he has helped to keep alive the memory of a splendid cricketer and also a man of the people.

Introduction by JACK SOKELL, Hon. Secretary of Wombwell Cricket Lovers Society and Yorkshire County Cricket Club Committee member.

EARLY DAYS IN WOMBWELL

'Wombwell is a large village and township formed into a parish from that of Darfield Jan 8, 1864 situated on the river Dove and on the Dearne and Dove canal, with a station on the Manchester, Sheffield and Lincolnshire railway, 1½ miles south-west of Darfield, 4 south-east from Barnsley, 7 north-west from Rotherham, 12 north from Sheffield and 169 from London and is in the Barnsley division of the Riding, Northern division of the wapentake of Staincross and Tickhill, Staincross petty sessional division, Barnsley union and county court district, rural deanery of Wath, archdeaconry of Sheffield and diocese of York . . .'

That was how Kelly's West Riding Directory of 1889 described the village of Wombwell in South Yorkshire, one year before the birth of, perhaps its most famous son, Yorkshire and England cricketer Roy Kilner.

Wombwell itself, had been basically a farming community until the advent of the Industrial Revolution, which swept through the country. Rapid growth saw Wombwell develop into a busy coal-mining village and with the sinking of mineshafts so the population increased at an equally rapid rate as people came from all over in search of work.

In 1881 the population of Wombwell stood at 8,451 by 1889 that number had increased to around 10,000 and before the turn of the century the figure had reached almost 17,000.

It was around this time that Seth Kilner, a native of Huddersfield, arrived in Wombwell like so many others in search of employment in one of the village's several mines. Mitchell Main and Wombwell Main were both in the village boundaries whilst nearby lay Darfield Main and Lundhill Colliery. Seth gained a place with Mitchell Main.

Local rivalry between the two pits, Mitchell Main and Wombwell Main was always keen, never more so than in their sporting confrontations be it cricket or soccer they were deadly rivals desperate not to lose. It was not uncommon for crowds of over 2,000 to be present whenever the two sides met. Seth quickly became involved in the sporting activity of the pit as a valuable member of both the cricket and soccer elevens. During his younger days in Huddersfield he had played cricket for the famous village side, Lascelles Hall, which could boast both Yorkshire and England cricketers having represented them over the years. Indeed Wilfred Rhodes encountered Seth Kilner when playing for Kirkheaton and remembered him as a good bowler.

Irving Washington was another member of the Mitchell Main XI who possessed obvious talent. A left-handed batsman he first played for Mitchell at the tender age of 15 and by the late 1890s had attracted the attention of the Yorkshire authorities. For a while he combined his studies as a mining engineer with that of cricket but when his chance came in the Yorkshire first eleven in 1900 he was so impressed with the likes of George Hirst and Schofield Haigh that he informed his father of his desire to become a professional cricketer. He didn't really establish himself in the Yorkshire ranks until 1902 when he scored over 1,000 runs in the season and recorded his first and sadly his only first-class century, 100 not out against Surrey at Headingley.

Ill-health forced him out of the game. He spent two years in South Africa in the hope of regaining his health. Whilst out there he played for Griqualand West in 1904–5 and Transvaal in 1906–7 but never again played for Yorkshire.

Seth Kilner and Irving Washington became good team mates and also very good friends. Seth also became a good friend of Irving's family. Irving's father, William, was the general manager of the Mitchell Main Colliery. It came as no real surprise therefore when Seth married Irving's sister, Mary Alice Washington.

A small cottage in the Littlefield Lane area close to the Mitchell family residence, Netherwood Hall, was Seth and Mary's first home. It was situated about a mile from the centre of Wombwell and it was here in 1889 that Mary gave birth to their first child, a boy they named Bernard Washington Kilner.

A year later, on 17th October 1890 their second child was born, another boy whom they named Roy. Shortly afterwards the family moved to Rose Cottage which was opposite Hawthorn Cottage where Irving Washington lived. Hawthorn Cottage overlooked the Mitchell Main cricket ground and was on Netherwood Road.

By 1891, Seth Kilner had taken over as captain of the cricket eleven and from the record that remains of that season he did a splendid job as Mitchell Main skipper. Seventeen matches were played of which ten were won with five draws and only two defeats, not a bad record.

Growing up in such a cricketing atmosphere Roy was encouraged to play the game by his father and by his Uncle Irving. From an early age it

The once famous Mitchell Main ground which saw many of Roy Kilner's early triumphs but in later years it was taken over by the Coal Board, sadly today it is a very barren and bleak place.

was clear to see that not only was he going to be another left handed batsman like his Uncle but that he also had an abundance of natural talent. Cricket in the summer months, soccer during the winter, Roy's childhood days probably consisted of very little else, they didn't need to.

The Kilner family was a large but happy one, Seth and his wife eventually brought up no less than eleven children, 7 sons and four daughters. Seth was a strict but fair father, woe betide any of the boys if they were heard using bad language. All the children attended Wombwell Parish Church, some of the family were in the choir and the boys were all at sometime or other members of the Church Lads Brigade.

All the boys learnt their cricket with Mitchell Main, it was simply a way of life. J. Belshaw, the then Chairman of Wombwell Urban Council, was associated with Roy when he was a boy and for sometime lived next door to the family:

'Kilner played cricket from morning till night and often his mother would fetch him off the pitch after dark.'

Norman Kilner, Roy's younger brother by 5 years who would later join him in the Yorkshire ranks before moving onto a successful career at Warwickshire, recalled his early childhood days during a conversation with Rob Brooke which appeared in an early edition of The Association of Cricket Statisticians journal *The Cricket Statistician*:

'We did not exactly learn our cricket in the streets because when I was a boy it was all country around Wombwell and we played in the fields. There was a football pitch across the road from where we lived and we often used that. There was no grass on it at all and we stuck anything up for wickets. If we had no bat we took a paling off the fence, sawed a bit off and used that. Balls were usually easy to come by. There was a private cricket club next door and when the players were practising we used to stand in the road waiting for one to come over the top. Someone was posted about 80 yards up the road, the ball was thrown up to him and he was off. There was a Polo field nearby and if we couldn't get a cricket ball we tried to get one of these. They are slightly larger than a cricket ball, solid wood and not quite round. We used to grab one and run.'

At the age of 14, Roy made his debut for the Mitchell Main XI against Swinton on 2nd September in a Mexborough league clash. It didn't prove a particularly successful first outing, Kilner being dismissed for just 7 runs. He got a second opportunity on 16th September when Main met Wath C.C. but again he was out cheaply, this time for just 3 runs. In the two games he also bowled eight overs which cost him 33 runs although he did pick up two wickets.

The following season, 1906, saw Kilner given an extended run in the Mitchell Main side but still at the age of only 15 his inexperience was evident in almost every innings he played. His desire to play shots often

Irving Washington – a Yorkshire player between 1900 and 1902, robbed of his chance at the highest level through ill-health but the inspiration for the 'boy' Kilner. (Courtesy of Tony Woodhouse.)

got him out and his highest score during the summer was 15. With only 81 runs to show from 15 innings, 2 not outs he ended the season with a batting average of 6.23, frustrating indeed for such a talented youngster. His bowling did at least progress, in all he had eleven victims at a cost of 12.09 each from 42 overs of slow left-arm.

His poor batting form in 1906 meant that he was pushed further down the order during the following season and it was instead his bowling which continued to attract greatest attention. His natural free-hitting style of approach to batsmanship linked with his lack of experience meant that he still continued to give his wicket away before he was properly set. That however was how he had learnt the game and it was his style, a style which would remain the same throughout the course of his career. His highest score in 1907 was 18 not out against Wath, whilst his eight wickets cost 109 runs at 13.62 apiece.

Still refusing to graft for his runs, his batting progressed very little in 1908. In 12 innings he scored 85 runs, 33 of those in one innings against Rawmarsh. Yet again he bowled more overs than in previous years, eighty in all and he handled that responsibility much better doubling his tally of wickets to sixteen.

Suddenly in the summer of 1909 his batting talent emerged to the full, rendering what had happened in previous seasons as irrelevant. Consistency at last became part of his natural free-scoring game and by the middle of June his first century for Mitchell Main was in the score-book. That maiden century was part of a remarkable family performance. The opposition on June 19th were arch rivals Wombwell Main. When Irving Washington joined his nephew at the crease three wickets were already down with the score on 40. They then embarked upon a thrilling 4th wicket partnership which added 215 runs as Mitchell Main ran up 255 for three, both batsmen were unbeaten, Roy Kilner on 103 and Washington, the senior partner on 112. It was the beginning of a good run for Roy with the bat. He followed his century against Wombwell with scores of 62 against Rawmarsh at Mitchell Main, 45 at Hickleton and 68 not out versus Wath. On the bowling front his tally of wickets dropped considerably and were more expensive than in previous years costing 17.57 each. Yet his final 'allround' figures for the summer made impressive reading:

Innings	Not Outs	H.S.	Runs	Average
17	4	103*	448	34.46

Overs	Maidens	Runs	Wickets	Average
46	14	123	7	17.57

*signifies Not Out

Roy it seemed had come of age, his achievements in 1909 with Mitchell Main attracted the attentions of the Yorkshire C.C.C. authorities. The time had come to test his talent beyond the boundaries of his beloved Wombwell, sterner challengers awaited him.

THE RISE TO COUNTY HONOURS

Kilner started the 1910 season in exactly the same way in which he had ended the previous one. Against Barnsley he scored an unbeaten 100 out of a Mitchell Main total of 204 for three. His good form continued with scores of 42 versus Monk Bretton and 76 against South Kirby.

By the end of June, the interest shown by the county authorities brought him a call-up to the Yorkshire 2nd XI to face Surrey at Horley at the tender age of 19. The most important innings of his life up to that time was over before it had even begun, caught Sullivan, bowled Edwards for no score. Given an opportunity with the ball he ended with two wickets costing 13 runs from 7 steady overs. In the 2nd innings he regained some of his lost confidence making 18 not out.

Despite that early set back he played in all the remaining 2nd XI fixtures that season. His second match proved a bigger failure than the Surrey game. He scored 2 runs and had bowling figures of one for 81 from 7 overs. Nearer to home in the game at Rotherham against Cheshire he made 30 but was not called upon to bowl. Durham at Barnsley were the next opponents but again he failed to trouble the scorers. Even worse was to follow in the game against Lancashire in August. He bagged a 'pair' and failed to take a wicket in two short spells with the ball. Northumberland dismissed him in the match at Bridlington for 28 and 2.

His best performance of the season came at Stoke where he made 36 and 13 against Staffordshire, but he let himself down again with only 7 in the final match at Rotherham against Surrey. It was hardly an inspired start, an average of 12.50 per innings and three wickets at nearly 40 each. The transition from league to 2nd XI cricket had proved a difficult ordeal for the young Kilner.

Throughout the summer, when not involved with the 2nd team, he continued to contribute significantly for his local side, Mitchell Main. His early season performances were backed up with good half centuries against Denaby and the old rivals Wombwell Main. By the end of the summer he had accumulated 605 runs at an average of almost 32 per innings and his ten wickets cost him just over 17 apiece. That form and the signs at least of a great deal of unfulfilled potential convinced the Yorkshire authorities that he should be given further encouragement. He had played on one occasion for Harrogate C.C. in 1910 and impressed many with an innings of 78.

When the new season started in 1911, Kilner was allocated to the Harrogate club as a colt in order to gain experience and hopefully realise some of the obvious potential he had shown in the innings he had played for Harrogate the year before. He joined Redfearn and Dunnington as club professionals. His performances now began to take on a far healthier complexion, his raw natural talent combined with the greater responsibility brought his game on much quicker than it otherwise might have had he remained playing local league cricket. Jack Redfearn, the Harrogate Cricket Club groundsman and professional of the time, realised Roy had great possibilities:

'I took a great liking to the boy and felt that he would make a good allround player. He got in a lot of practice at Harrogate, and I think that stood him in very good stead in his later career with the county. He was a lad with a nice pleasant disposition, and popular with everybody.'

Yet despite his popularity and good humour he still continued to have good and bad days with the Yorkshire 2nds. In June of 1911 for example at Rotherham he made 34 and 0 against Lancashire. The story for Harrogate was totally different where he quickly made his presence felt with 102 not out against Bradford. His bowling also attracted attention with such feats as seven for 33 against Skipton at Harrogate.

Yorkshire lost their first Championship match of the season at Leyton against Essex under their new captain E. J. Radcliffe, in his first full season as skipper following the retirement of Lord Hawke. The side quickly made amends with victory over Derbyshire at Sheffield.

For the next match against Somerset at Taunton a new name was brought into the side, a player by the name of Roy Kilner. His first class debut proved as successful as his 2nd XI one had. The opportunity was wasted as he failed to trouble the Somerset bowlers and was again out without scoring. Yorkshire at least won the match comfortably.

Those two successive wins over Derbyshire and Somerset were followed by a further six triumphs over Worcestershire, Somerset, Derbyshire again, Lancashire, Warwickshire and Leicestershire. It was a run of success which carried Yorkshire to the top of the County Championship. Middlesex then beat them on a drying pitch at Lord's and the game against Kent at Bramhall Lane ended as a draw due to the weather which also spoilt the match against Northamptonshire. Defeat at the hands of Surrey set the pattern for the season, Yorkshire played inconsistently throughout and by the close had dropped to 7th place in the Championship table. They won only 3 of their last 12 games and were beaten in 5 of those.

For Kilner, his season very much followed the pattern of Yorkshire's, good times and bad. His duck against Somerset was followed by an equally poor run of low scores, 6 and 2 at Northampton, 12 and 3 not out against Worcester were typical efforts. In all he played 7 games for the first XI but failed to impress in any. His ten innings brought him 60 runs at an average of 6.66. His form with the 2nd team was also inconsistent, 119 against Surrey at The Oval in June was the highlight but again he followed it with nought in the 2nd innings. In his other game for the 2nds he made 10 and 27 against Keighley and Craven in August.

His overall figures for Harrogate, though, made for better reading, 519 runs at 37.07 and given more chances to bowl had 28 wickets to his name from 168 overs at an average of 13.42. His first team failures were somewhat compensated for by his good record for the North Yorkshire side. By the time the new season started in 1912 a new skipper was at the helm and a fresh start awaited the cheerful left-hander from Wombwell.

Sir Archibald White took over the reins of captaincy for the 1912 campaign, a position he held until the outbreak of World War One.

Early May proved to be wet, it set the pattern for the entire summer. Yorkshire opened their Championship fixtures with a nine wicket win at Leicestershire but the weather intervened in the match at Sheffield where Hampshire escaped with a draw. A similar result followed in the match with Kent at Leeds. After a weak Yorkshire XI were beaten by Cambridge at Fenners by 4 wickets, the full strength side had a comfortable 10 wicket win over Lancashire. Further frustration due to the rain resulted in a draw at Dewsbury against Somerset and then the abandonment of the match with Surrey at Sheffield. With a first innings lead of 139 over Essex at Huddersfield, Yorkshire were well placed to force home their advantage but the rain once again thwarted their progress, another depressing draw the end result.

Middlesex became the first (and as it would later turn out the only) side to beat Yorkshire in the Championship of 1912 by 4 wickets at Lord's. That defeat left them in 6th place in the Championship.

Despite losing the 2nd day to bad weather, Gloucestershire were beaten by 74 runs, being dismissed for 68 and 110 in their 2nd innings.

For the following game against Nottinghamshire at Trent Bridge, Kilner received a call-up and another chance to prove his undoubted ability. It was the end of June and the summer was proving wetter than most. George Hirst was injured and Roy's early season from fully justified giving him another opportunity in the first XI ranks. In May at The Oval he had scored 79 and 10 for the Yorkshire 2nds. During June he had been

The Yorkshire Championship side of 1912, a powerful unit led by Sir Archibald White. From left to right:
Back row: Dolphin, Booth, Drake, Rhodes, J. Hoyland (Scorer).
Middle Row: Wilson, Denton, Sir. A. W. White, Hirst, Haigh.
Front Row: Roy Kilner, Olroyd and Bates. (Courtesy of Tony Woodhouse.)

selected in a rain-ruined match against the Bradford Cricket League. He also played in two other 2nd XI games with a good deal of success. In the match at Ossett against Yorkshire Council he made 112 and then at Rotherham in the return with Surrey totally dominated proceedings scoring 136 and finishing with bowling figures of six for 41 in the 1st innings and six for 34 in the second. It was these performances linked with his continued consistency for Harrogate which earned him a deserved second chance.

On a good pitch, Nottinghamshire batted first and after having tried five bowlers, Kilner was called into the attack. This was how *The Field* described his bowling:

'Small and sturdy, but not quite as broad as the typical professional that the North and the Midlands have produced of late years, he bowls with the left hand, and is about as fast as Rhodes used to be. He has a short and practical run, a loose arm, and with an easy action can change his pace rather well.'

He came on to bowl 20 minutes before lunch with A. O. Jones and Hardstaff in command of the situation. Yet he kept them both very quiet and so White, the Yorkshire captain, allowed him to continue bowling with pleasing results. Nottinghamshire totalled 261 out of which Kilner had figures of four for 66. Yorkshire batted poorly and were bowled out for 145, Kilner failing to score. On a deteriorating pitch Nottinghamshire were all out for 132 leaving a target of 249 to win for Yorkshire. At 133 for 4 the game was in the balance but Kilner and J. Tasker, another youngster, added 113 for the fifth wicket with Tasker making 52 and Kilner a match winning contribution of 83 not out as Yorkshire won by 5 wickets. He had proved a more than adequate replacement for the injured Hirst.

His success at Trent Bridge kept him in the side even after the return to fitness of George Hirst. Two more drawn games against Northants at Bradford and Warwickshire at Birmingham were followed by a 214 run victory over Worcestershire at Dewsbury.

Yorkshire were in trouble at Bristol being 13 for 3 before Denton with 29 and Kilner 30, lifted the total to 134 all out. Gloucestershire finished only 2 runs in arrears but then Denton with 182 helped Yorkshire to 411 for nine declared and Gloucestershire were then bowled out for 166.

Kent and Leicestershire were easily beaten and Yorkshire moved into 2nd place in the Championship behind their next opponents, Northamptonshire. The poor weather which so plagued the summer intervened but not before Kilner had compiled 57 in Yorkshire's 1st innings.

Whilst the side continued to do well, Kilner was steadily trying to establish himself in a highly talented unit. Solid rather than spectacular performances characterised the remainder of his season. In Yorkshire's 88 all out at Hull he had the satisfaction of being top-scorer with 22 not out in a rain-ruined match.

The Mitchell Main football eleven circa 1910–13. Roy is pictured on the middle row, first on the left. Next to cricket Kilner's abiding passion was football. (Kind permission of Ken Sykes.)

Four wins in their last six matches gave Yorkshire their 6th Championship title since 1900 (their 9th in all) and their first since 1908. They had the satisfaction of knowing, they had won despite the fact that many of their home fixtures had been badly affected by the weather.

Denton finished on top of the batting averages with over 2,000 runs and Haigh was the leading bowler with 125 wickets at 12.06 each. Major Booth, a good friend of Kilner's, finished 2nd with 104 wickets.

In his first full season of first-class cricket, Kilner could be considered a minor success. From the Nottinghamshire match onwards he had held a regular first-team place and he ended the season having played 23 matches and scored 570 runs at 22.80, his 16 wickets cost him 21.12 each. At Harrogate he continued to do well, 107 against Kings Cross was backed up by splendid bowling such as seven for 15 against Bowling Old Lane and five for 24 versus Leeds Springfield. In all he made 370 runs at 37 per innings and bagged 40 wickets at only 7.5 apiece.

In the winter months Kilner returned to Wombwell where he played soccer with Mitchell Main. His talent for sport was not solely restricted to the cricket field for he was also an outstanding soccer player. He possessed a long throw from the touch-line which was known to reach the goal mouth on many occasions. In later life he would play at right-back for Preston North End and he also turned out in a few games for Barnsley as a wing-half.

The return of cricket in 1913 saw Kilner beginning his first full season as a regular first team member. His last game for the 2nd XI had been played in 1912 where he finished on a high note, 337 runs from 4 innings played at an average of 84.25. Another connection was also severed during the summer of 1913 as Kilner played his last game for Harrogate, not batting at all for them and bowling just 14 overs which cost him 33 runs whilst collecting three wickets. His time with the club, as a colt, had proved invaluable and time well spent. Between 1910 and 1913 he had scored 967 runs at an average of 38.68 and taken 71 wickets costing just under 10 apiece.

The opening fixture of the new season began with defeat against the 'old enemy' at Old Trafford by an innings and 3 runs, Heap taking 11 wickets in the match for Lancashire.

Back to something like form, Yorkshire then beat Gloucestershire at Bristol and followed this up with an innings win over Somerset with Booth and Drake the dominant bowlers.

Kilner's first significant contribution of the new season came at Fenners where, after Yorkshire had made 266, Rhodes 102, Cambridge took a first innings lead of 74, Rhodes seven for 98 virtually producing a 'one man' performance. Yorkshire's 2nd innings was a far better effort as they reached 361 for 7 declared, Alonzo Drake scoring 108 in a partnership of

175 for the 5th wicket with Kilner who struck 77.

Moving to Bradford for the game against Kent, Kilner figured in an even more important century partnership, this time with George Hirst. In a closely contested match, Kent left the home side needing 310 to win in 5 hours and at 41 for four, Yorkshire seemed destined for defeat but then Hirst and Kilner came together and in poor light added an unbroken 151 for the 5th wicket, Hirst leading the charge with 102 not out. When the rain came with 70 minutes of play left, Yorkshire were 192 for 4 with young Kilner 50 not out.

Trent Bridge was the next port of call and Yorkshire began the game well making 471 in their 1st innings with, once again, Kilner in splendid form this time 76 to his name but still unable to reach that elusive first century. Denton it was who the stole the show with 148. Gunn scored 132 and 109 not out as Nottinghamshire comfortably saved the game.

The match against Leicestershire at Headingley could not have started any worse from a Yorkshire viewpoint, at one stage being 58 for 5. This time though Kilner grasped the opportunity and in a fluent partnership with his friend, Major Booth, added 184 in 110 minutes. Kilner went on to make his first century in first class cricket, 104. More importantly he had done so at a vital time for his side. It was his 4th century partnership in consecutive matches. Hirst with ten for 48 helped Yorkshire to win by an innings and 108 runs.

The hero of Wombwell came quickly down to earth in the next match once again failing to trouble the scorers at Leyton against Essex. The ups and downs of cricket were proving even greater at county level. He took his failures heavily on himself and did not need to be told by his captain when an error had been made. At least he had the consolation of knowing that despite his own poor match his side won by 3 wickets and then went on to crush Worcestershire at Fartown by 213 runs in the next game.

Roy showed the value of his hitting ability when required in the game at Sheffield. After Yorkshire had made 254, Booth, with six for 84, left Warwickshire trailing by 102 runs. Kilner then led the run charge with 74 made in only 55 minutes leaving Warwickshire a target of 298 to win. Hirst with five wickets gave his side victory by 89 runs.

The next game at Northampton was drawn but their wins over Somerset and Leicestershire were obtained without any significant contribution from the cheerful Wombwell player. But in the return against Northants Kilner made another important impression. On a helpful pitch Northamptonshire made 145, Rhodes seven wickets. Yorkshire then fell apart for 107, Haywood and Seymour with half centuries gave Northants a lead of 232. At 56 for 4 the game seemed all but over. Hirst and Kilner, though, added 74 for the 5th wicket to put them back in the hunt. Pullin later made the comment:

Kilner taking strike – 'After a usually shaky start he would play attractive and at times dashing cricket. His best strokes included the off-drive and the hook.' (Courtesy of Tony Woodhouse.)

'Yorkshire were always winning while Kilner was at the wicket . . .' And so it seemed but when he had reached 91, S. G. Smith gave him a short delivery which he pulled in the air to George Thompson at deep square-leg who had been positioned for such a shot. With Kilner gone, Yorkshire subsided from 199 for 7 to 212 all out losing the game by 20 runs. Yet still it had been a splendid effort from Kilner.

His good form continued at Harrogate where opening the batting he struck 85 as Yorkshire beat Hampshire by 182 runs although Hampshire did miss eight catches.

A fifty at Edgbaston in a drawn game with Warwickshire, 94 against Middlesex at Sheffield and 85 at Bradford against Essex proved to many that here was yet another solid and reliable batsman. It was a bright finish to a successful summer.

Yorkshire finished in 2nd position in the Championship behind Kent although there were those who felt the side of 1913 had played generally better than the team which had won the Championship the previous year.

Over 1500 runs at an average of 34.47 must have brought a broad smile to the face of Kilner. He had scored his first century for Yorkshire and had 12 other innings of 50 or more to reflect upon. He finished just behind George Hirst at the head of the averages. His bowling had been used very sparingly and in total he added only 2 more wickets to his tally taken in 1912. The bowling part of his game served merely as a second string to his bow, with so much talent available in the side on the bowling front he had been called upon very little.

The same could not be said of his batting which had matured and prospered. Several times during the season he had played a major part in helping his side out of difficulty and once or twice his efforts had won the day for his county. Early in an innings, Kilner would be impatient, flicking at balls outside his off-stump that he had no need to play at, a typical left-hander's trait. Yet after a usually shaky start he would play attractive and, at times, dashing cricket. His best strokes included the off-drive and the hook-shot which he played particularly well and with powerful wrists was able to square-cut with immense force. Like his important contributions in 1913 many of his best innings were played when his side were in deep trouble and needed him most.

THE WAR YEARS

During the winter of 1913–14, Roy was struck down by a serious illness. From this distance in time it is impossible to discover exactly what, but it was serious enough to affect his form somewhat when the new first-class season got underway in 1914.

His splendid batting form the previous summer had established him as a first-choice player, popular not only with his fellow team mates but liked and admired from a distance by Yorkshire supporters for his light-hearted, friendly and joyful approach to the game.

The last summer of the era known in cricket history as 'The Golden Age' began full of optimism certainly from a Yorkshire point of view, for although Schofield Haigh had played his last game and both Hirst and Denton were advanced in years, the nucleus of a new young side was emerging with both Booth and Drake as top-class allrounders. With Kilner, Wilson and Percy Holmes to provide the batting strength for years to come it seemed the hopes of a new era for Yorkshire cricket were well founded. Sadly by the time autumn had arrived, the world was embarking on a bloody path and it was war not cricket which became a way of life. Yorkshire's young men together with the rest of the country would soon be fighting another battle on foreign shores, many would not return.

Sir Archibald White was once again Yorkshire captain when the Championship campaign got underway at Northampton with a win. The visitors made 378, Denton 58 and Kilner, at this stage showing no signs of the illness which had laid him low, made 77. Northamptonshire were shot out for 117 and 105 with Hirst, six for 34, and Drake, six for 40, taking the bowling honours.

The M.C.C. were brushed aside being dismissed for 39 and 134, Booth in magnificent early season form picking up figures of seven for 21 and four for 21. This 'golden spell' continued at Leyton where he shot Essex out with six for 96 and eight for 64.

Hampshire brought Yorkshire's winning run to an end with a draw at Southampton. Phil Mead scoring 213 whilst Denton, 168 not out, and Hirst 146 saved the day for Yorkshire.

Their first actual defeat of the season came at Bradford against Surrey. In a close game dominated by Hobbs, 100 and 74, and Rhodes, six for 109, 89 and then five for 56, the visitors ran out winners by 28 runs.

After his early success in the game at Northampton, the effects of his winter illness had taken their toll and Kilner had featured very little in Yorkshire's batting performances. Forty eight and seventeen in Yorkshire's defeat by Surrey had suggested a more consistent pattern and that proved correct in the Roses match that followed at Bramhall Lane where, on a good wicket, Kilner top-scored with 93 out of his side's total of 381. Lancashire made 370 but after Yorkshire declared on 252 for 9 there was not enough time left to force a result, Lancashire ending on 130 for two.

Leicestershire provided the next opposition but rain intervened and the match ended without any positive result for either side. Rhodes at his very best took seven for 19 to give Yorkshire an unexpected victory over Derbyshire at Headingley.

Rain forced a draw with Warwickshire, but not before Crowther Charlesworth had scored 206.

Poor batting led to defeat at the hands of Kent at Tonbridge and Yorkshire's 'bad run' continued with four draws and a second defeat at the hands of Kent.

Hirst was carrying an injury which naturally weakened the side and Kilner had not fully shaken off the effects of his winter illness. On 30th June he turned out for Mitchell Main in the hope of regaining some of his lost confidence and form, but he made only 27 before being dismissed in the game with Darfield. He had played one other match for the Main side in early April against Rotherham in which he had compiled a splendid 102 not out. Since that innings he had failed to regain his best form and fitness.

The game at Bramhall Lane where Yorkshire lost for a second time to Kent brought the turn-around in Kilner's form. Yorkshire were reduced to 44 for 5 on a wicket affected by rain, but Kilner, as he did so often when it mattered, came to his side's rescue with a marvellous cameo fifty out of Yorkshire's 101 all out. Kent did little better and finished only 25 runs ahead on 1st innings but Blythe, eight for 55, then bowled Yorkshire out for 105 and Kent won by 5 wickets. Yorkshire's poor run left them in 12th position in the Championship.

On the first day at Huddersfield Yorkshire made 346 thanks to Rhodes with 59 and Kilner 79. Both were overshadowed by Hirst who hit 105 not out in 3 hours. The game was over by the end of the second day, Northamptonshire crumbled against Booth, seven for 69 which gave Yorkshire victory by an innings and 8 runs. The revival had begun.

'Lonzo' Drake took Yorkshire to an unlikely win over Derbyshire at Chesterfield when he took four wickets in four successive balls, finishing with five for 6 from 3 overs as Derbyshire's last six wickets fell with the score on 68.

Wins over Nottinghamshire and Somerset kept up Yorkshire's challenge and Kilner with 79 in a partnership with Wilson, (102) of 119 for the 3rd wicket helped Yorkshire to make 449 in the match with Gloucestershire which was also won.

Lancashire were easily beaten at Old Trafford and at Edgbaston, Warwickshire were beaten inside two days by 163 runs. Yorkshire started badly and were 4 for two when Kilner and Denton came together and in a thrilling partnership saw Yorkshire past the hundred mark in less than an hour. Denton made 60 and Kilner 50 out of their sides 243. Drake dismissed the home side for 110 and, on a pitch giving increasing assistance to the bowlers, Warwickshire were all out for 96 in their second innings, Major Booth taking five for 39. A two-wicket win over Middlesex gave Yorkshire their 8th successive win and lifted them to 4th place in the table.

Yorkshire's winning sequence ended in the next game against Surrey. The match was played at Lord's as The Oval had been taken over by the military authorities. The realities of war were drawing near and the game was played in a strange atmosphere, more important things than cricket were now beginning to occupy the minds of spectators and players alike. Surrey ran up a massive total of 549 for six, Hayward 116, Hobbs 202 and Hayes 134. Despite Yorkshire's run of success they seemed disinterested in the game and were bowled out for 204 and 315, losing by an innings and 30 runs. In their second innings Kilner made 54 along with a half-century from Denton and 95 from Wilson.

A return to winning ways came at Bradford as Sussex were beaten by an innings and 183 runs, Kilner, 55, forming another good partnership, this time 110 with B. B. Wilson for the 3rd wicket. Wilson batted over 5½ hours for his eventual 208 out of Yorkshire's 443.

Yet another innings victory came at Bristol as Gloucestershire were bowled out for only 94, Booth, six for 48, and Drake, four for 41, bowled unchanged. When Yorkshire batted Wilson made 56 but Kilner played even better. His second first-class century proved a faultless display. He hit powerfully on the leg-side and drove the ball well in making 169. He added 117 for the sixth wicket with Holmes, 61, in only 75 minutes. Booth and Drake again bowled unchanged in Gloucestershire's 2nd innings, Booth collected six victims and Drake four as the home side collapsed to 84 all out.

Kilner failed completely in the match at Weston-super-Mare making 4 and 2 but the headlines belonged to Alonzo Drake who became the first Yorkshire bowler to take all ten wickets in an innings. He finished with ten for 35 and match figures of 15 for 51 having again bowled unchanged with Booth.

Yorkshire's last match of the season, and what would later prove to be their last game for five long years, was at Brighton against Sussex. The war was on the minds of most and cricket was largely forgotten. Before the match. A. W. Pullin spoke to both Roy Kilner and his good friend and team mate Major Booth. He later recalled that conversation in his *History of Yorkshire County Cricket 1903 to 1923*:

'When the players were assembling for the game at Brighton, I had a conversation with Major Booth and Roy Kilner, and they told me they had decided to enlist directly they returned home. Major added – "It is our duty, Mr Pullin; we cannot do anything else." '

The final match with Sussex ended in a draw and along with Booth and Arthur Dolphin, Kilner left for home and then to enlist in the Leeds and Bradford 'Pals' Battalion in the West Yorkshire Regiment.

Yorkshire, for the record, finished the season in fourth place in the Championship behind Surrey, Middlesex and Kent. The matches scheduled against an England XI at Harrogate and M.C.C. at Scarborough were both abandoned because of the war.

Hirst was top of the batting averages with 1655 runs at 41.37. Denton who scored 1799 runs was in 2nd spot. Kilner despite his poor form at various stages of the season had rediscovered his best form towards the close and still ended with 1329 runs at 30.90, one century and eleven scores of 50 or more. His bowling was seldom used, in fact he bowled only 84 overs during the season and had taken only one wicket which cost him 305 runs.

The batting and bowling averages for 1914 were quickly forgotten as the men, some still only boys, left their families and loved ones behind to fight for their country. Roy Kilner and Major Booth were stationed at Colsterdale in North Yorkshire with the Leeds City Battalion but in early November 1914 both returned to Wombwell for a special occasion.

The wedding of Roy Kilner and Miss Annie Camplejohn took place at Wombwell Parish Church. Set against the background of war it must have been a strange atmosphere of joy and sadness for soon both Kilner and his best man Booth would be fighting in France.

The bride was the third daughter of Mr James Camplejohn, engineer of the Darfield Main Collieries at Darfield Main. The bridegroom had returned home for the ceremony only that morning having obtained a few precious days' leave. Both Kilner and Major Booth were in uniform and Gordon Kilner (Roy's younger brother) acted as groomsman. The bride was given away by her father and she was attended by two bridesmaids, her sister Miss Eleanor Camplejohn and Roy's sister Dorothy Kilner.

The previous evening Roy and his best man had been given a rousing send-off from Colsterdale by his comrades of the 'B' Company of the Leeds Battalion. In honour of the forthcoming occasion the two soldiers were fitted out in their uniforms. Immediately after the parade at half-past four, a section of 'B' Company rushed for Kilner and carried him shoulder high past the sentry to waiting transport which took him to Masham, six miles away, where the last train was due to depart at 5.50 that evening. Amid ringing cheers a great deal of confetti was hurled at the popular Yorkshire cricketer and Booth, towering high above Kilner, also came in for attention with the confetti throwers.

Kilner's leave began that Thursday evening, it included his wedding day and three days following. He reported back to Colsterdale the following Monday, it had been happiness for far too brief a time.

The next four years held in store much tragedy for Kilner and his family, the war brought suffering and misery to many and the Kilners would not be excluded from such pain.

During a brief period at home in 1915, Kilner played for Mitchell Main in three games. He batted in them all and had scores of only 21, 18 and 1. He bowled 24 overs and took 12 wickets for 48 runs. His mind was not on cricket but such enjoyable times had to be cherished for they were few and far between. Another bright light in the darkness was the birth of the Kilners' first child, a son they named Roy junior.

The first part of the war saw Roy serving for the 'Pals' in Egypt. Injury forced him home but he was quickly back on active duty and the call came, inevitably perhaps, to leave for France and the Western Front. Major Booth by now had become a 2nd Leiutenant and both he and Kilner were involved in the bloody events which later became known as the 'Somme'.

On the 1st July 1916, Booth was killed in action near La Cigny (Lens). He was only 29 years of age. One of the most promising allrounders of the pre-war era was dead. In an all too brief career between 1908 and 1914 he had scored over 4,000 runs and taken in excess of 550 wickets. It was not only a grave loss to Yorkshire but to English cricket. No one grieved more than Roy Kilner. He and Major Booth had been good friends even before they had been together in the Yorkshire ranks. Booth, although originally from Pudsey, qualified as an electrician and had worked in Wath at a local colliery. He became captain of Wath Athletic Club, then playing in the Mexborough league, and it was there that he and Kilner had first encountered one another, Kilner being the 'young star' of the Mitchell Main side. Their friendship had grown over the years, Booth being Roy's best man at his wedding only 2 years before his untimely death. They were friends until the very end, for Corporal Kilner was fighting in the same action in which Booth was killed. Roy was lucky to escape with his life for he was a casualty before the onslaught by the 'Pals' occurred. He was in the assembly trenches prior to the advance when he received a wound in his right wrist from shrapnel whilst carrying bombs around.

His injury required a period of convalescence and so he was brought home and moved to a military hospital at Squires Gate near Blackpool. When his condition improved he was assigned to Preston Garrison and

Roy Kilner suffered, as many others did, the effects of World War I but here he is pictured during one of the brighter moments, at home from the war with his first son, Roy junior. (Reproduced from The Cricketers of Wombwell.*)*

The White Rose formerly the Halfway House, the one-time home of Seth Kilner and his family. The yard on the left of the photograph is probably one of the most famous in cricket being the place where Roy Kilner practised and developed his bowling skills in the years that followed the 1914–18 War.

there his services as a mechanic for which he had been originally trained were used to best effect.

Football had always been next to cricket, one of Kilner's abiding passions and it was during his period in the North West that he turned out for Preston North End F.C. In the booklet *Cricketers of Wombwell* it states that he played at right-back for the club partnering the Lancashire cricketer, Billy Cook. Having consulted with the Club historian, Ian Rigby, he is unable to trace any record of Billy Cook having played at the same time and there is no player by the name of Kilner or Smith (which was the assumed name he sometimes used to avoid detection in the side) for the season 1916–17. One can only assume he was too ill at that stage to have been actively involved on the football field.

The first actual reference to Kilner having played is in 1918, September 28th in the game against Liverpool where he is named as the right-back. One point of interest is that on November 16th against Manchester United, the right-back is given in the local newspaper as both Kilner and Smith! Very few clear records remain of his footballing performances with Preston, what is clear though is that had he not made the grade as a cricketer he may well have done so as a professional football player.

By the end of 1918 the war, thankfully, was over. Like so many families the Kilners had known the sadness of losing people dear to their hearts. Not only had Kilner lost his good friend Major Booth but in October 1917 his eldest brother Bernard Washington Kilner had been killed in the battle of Ypres aged only 27. The eldest of the Kilner family, who in his brief life had been another naturally gifted sportsman, received the Meritorious Service Medal for his bravery.

The tragedy of war behind them, it was time to try and readjust to a 'normal' way of life in an inevitably changed world. The 'Golden Age' of innocence had passed and had been replaced instead with a new harshness and determination. Cricket would shortly return but that too would be changed by the events of war. For Kilner there were new challengers to face for he would now be regarded as one of the experienced Yorkshire players. A far greater burden would rest on his broad shoulders but still his smiling face would always prevail.

FROM BATSMAN TO ALLROUNDER 1919 to 1923

Yorkshire cricket suffered as much as most other counties the after effects of the war. The loss of Major Booth was followed, a few short months before cricket was due to recommence again, by the death of another rising star of the pre-war days, Alonzo Drake, the left-handed allrounder from Honley near Huddersfield. He was only 34 when heart trouble combined with cancer of the throat ended his life in February 1919. To add to those two tragic losses Kilner himself was still recovering from the injury he had sustained in battle and four years without cricket had robbed some players of years they could never replace due to their age. Benny Wilson was 39 and too slow in the field to be of use, his services were dispensed with. George Hirst was 48 and had only 2 further seasons of cricket left in him, retiring in 1921 (although his final appearance was in 1929), Rhodes was 42 yet his career would continue another 11 years. Sir Archibald White had retired from the captaincy and was replaced by D. C. F. Burton, an enthusiastic leader.

A new system of cricket welcomed the players' return. The advocates of two-day Championship cricket (of which there were very few in Yorkshire) had got their way and so the first post-war season saw matches played over two days' duration with the hours of play being long and demanding on the players, a normal day began at 11.30 a.m. and ended at 7.30 p.m., the title to be decided by the percentage of wins to matches played. It proved a highly unpopular and unsuccessful experiment which was quickly abandoned in time for the return of 3-day fixtures in 1920.

1919 was a dry summer which to some extent helped the 2-day idea but still the lack of time meant that 56 out of 124 games ended in draws.

Yorkshire took the field for the first game against Gloucestershire with a new-look side. Sutcliffe had never played before, Blackburn and Claughton only once and E. Smith could boast three appearances. The captain, Burton, and Holmes also had very few first XI appearances to speak of and both had yet to establish themselves. The old guard was represented by Rhodes and Hirst with Denton, Dolphin and Kilner being the other instantly recognisable names. An innings victory over Gloucestershire was the perfect start for Yorkshire and Kilner who quickly found his form with his third first class hundred, 112, he and Rhodes having added 165 for the 3rd wicket.

A draw with Essex was followed by defeat at the hands of Lancashire at Old Trafford by 140 runs. Warwickshire were beaten with ease at Edgbaston as were Derbyshire, beaten by 10 wickets at Bradford.

Several new players were tried during the season, some who would become household names, Sutcliffe, Emmott Robinson and Abe Waddington and for the match at Sheffield against Nottinghamshire a familiar sounding name, Norman Kilner, Roy's younger brother, was brought into the side. He scored 39 in the 2nd innings but played in only two other matches that summer without success. His association with Yorkshire was to prove far shorter than Roy's. Maurice Leyland eventually won the battle for the batting spot Norman had tried to make his own. He scored two centuries for Yorkshire before leaving to join Warwickshire in 1924 where he stayed until 1937 making over 17,000 runs in his career. Nottinghamshire won the game at Sheffield by 6 wickets and three draws against Kent, Derbyshire and Nottinghamshire left Yorkshire with a lot of ground to make up.

Six of the next 7 Championship matches were won lifting them into 1st place in the table. Kilner's 2nd century of the season came in the return match with Gloucestershire at Headingley where he made 115 not out.

Sussex became the 3rd side to beat Yorkshire in 1919 by 5 wickets at Harrogate but innings victories against Leicestershire and Warwickshire kept Yorkshire at the head of the Championship table. Their last four games were all interrupted by rain and resulted in draws. Had Kent beaten Middlesex in their last match it would have cost Yorkshire the title but they failed to do so and Yorkshire were crowned Champions for the 10th time. Sutcliffe, in his first season, topped the batting averages and Rhodes the bowling with 142 wickets. Kilner once again passed the 1,000 run mark and in all scored three centuries added to his two against Gloucestershire he also made 120 at Lord's in the match with the M.C.C. On the bowling front the loss of Drake and Booth meant that he bowled far more than previously, getting through 377.3 overs, his 45 wickets were taken at a very respectable 18.31. He also played his first match for the Players against the Gentlemen in 1919. Like so many of his first matches at different levels he failed to score, dismissed by his Yorkshire colleague E. R. Wilson. He bowled in both innings without success but at least was accurate. The Players won the match at Scarborough by an innings and

110 runs. His next appearance in such matches would not come until July 1923.

1920

The return of 3-day Championship cricket in 1920 brought immediate success for Yorkshire with 7 wins from their first 8 matches. The first came against Derbyshire at Sheffield by an innings and 223 runs in a match which proved memorable for Roy Kilner.

Out of Yorkshire's total of 419 for 6 declared, Kilner passed his previous best score of 169 made against Gloucestershire in 1914 and went on to finish with 206 not out. One local newspaper described the innings thus: 'Kilner was in brilliant form, and off-drove with great power and pulled the ball to the leg boundary with infinite ease . . . Kilner was undefeated on 206 and he had batted five minutes short of four hours in compiling his total. His display was a brilliant one, and apart from a hard chance when in the 50s it was without blemish. He batted confidently and made his runs with all manner of well executed strokes through showing his usual partiality for hits on the leg side.'

Derbyshire were dismissed for 103 and 93, Rhodes picking up match figures of five for 15 from 24 overs with 14 maidens. Kilner also picked up two wickets for only 3 runs in the first innings to round off a very enjoyable game from his point of view. That innings of 206 would remain the highest first-class score of his career.

A fine game of cricket at Bradford saw Yorkshire emerge as the eventual winners by the slender margin of 22 runs over Lancashire in a Roses match to remember. Easy victories against Warwickshire, Gloucestershire, Worcestershire and a ten-wicket win over Nottinghamshire lifted Yorkshire towards the title leadership and with Middlesex escaping with a draw thanks only to the stubborn batting of Hearne and Hendren, it seemed they were set for retaining the Championship. Another crushing win over Essex by 206 runs at Dewsbury seemed merely to confirm that, but they met with their first defeat in the following game, beaten by Surrey at Sheffield due in large part to the batting of Jack Hobbs (112 and 70).

The marvellous early season run was replaced by inconsistency, a win over Leicestershire, defeat at the hands of Hampshire and a draw with Kent at Sheffield.

Roy continued to bat consistently during the summer making 121 against Warwickshire and 137 in the match with Nottinghamshire. Typical fighting innings from the plucky Wombwell player were also a feature of his game, 79 at Maidstone in a partnership of 140 with Denton failed to save his side from another defeat.

The Championship hopes of Yorkshire were now dispelled and at the close of the season it was Middlesex who were crowned as Champions with Lancashire second, Surrey in third and Yorkshire fourth.

Holmes finished top of the averages and Kilner was second with 1,316 runs at 36.55. His tally of wickets were considerably down on 1919, 27 wickets at the slightly expensive 25.33. The critics might have said he was under bowled and certainly Wilfred Rhodes was of that opinion. With his advancing years, the need to find back-up in the slow left-arm department was vitally important. Rhodes felt the task would be best undertaken by far greater use of Roy Kilner. His recommendation to Roy, that he should go away during the winter leave and work on his bowling skills, would ultimately transform Kilner from a batsman who sometimes bowled into a genuine allround cricketer.

Seth Kilner and the rest of the Kilner family were by now living in the Halfway House Hotel in Wombwell where Seth had taken over as landlord. The yard of the Hotel became Roy's practice area where he worked constantly on his bowling in order to improve it to a level where it would be regarded as a real force in the first class game. Norman Kilner recalled those memorable days in the yard to Rob Brooke:

'When we were professionals my brother Roy and I laid a concrete pitch in the yard of the Halfway House, the hotel in Wombwell where our father lived, and some of the Yorkshire players would come along and we used to play matches. My father and my uncle Irving used to captain the two teams, which sometimes had to be made up by my two sisters, and each player would pay sixpence, the winning team taking all. We chalked a wicket on the wall of the yard. That wall must be the most famous in cricket – there were sometimes eight England players playing there. The yard of the Halfway House served as our winter cricket school.'

Another person who recalls those special days in the backyards close to the Kilner home is Mrs K Bell, a local Wombwell resident:

'I remember how the Guest boys from next door and the two Atkin boys used to join in with those in the other 2 yards and supposedly get up a list of donations for a cricket bat, knowing full well that Roy would give them one when he was at home. The local children also had another ploy; if they played in the backyards or as a special treat on the concrete yard of the Halfway House any damage done, young Roy junior would claim to have done it, and his father would pay.'

Jack Varney, one of those young boys, quickly realised why Roy Kilner was so popular:

'Roy was a very generous man, always fair and always smiling.'

1921

With the birth of their second son, Major, whom they named after Major

Booth, the Kilners moved to 212 Barnsley Road in Wombwell situated not far from the Halfway House.

The Kilners and the family next door became close friends. Alice Lindley was an excellent cook and when Roy was at home he could be found in her kitchen sampling some of her home made chips of which he was particularly fond.

Away from family life, the Championship again evaded Yorkshire in 1921 as Middlesex took the title, Surrey were 2nd and Yorkshire improved one place from 1920 to finish in 3rd position.

For the Kilner brothers it was a pleasing summer. Norman scored his first century for the county, 112 against Leicestershire whilst Roy seemed very keen on the Northamptonshire bowling with scores of 166 and 150 against them. In the match at Harrogate he and Holmes added 299 for the 4th wicket having put on 276 with Rhodes for the 5th wicket in the game at Northampton. Certainly Northamptonshire felt the full effect of Kilner's bat during a summer which saw his bowling also emerge from the shadows. He again completed 1,000 runs for the season but even more pleasing was his tally of wickets, 61 at 18.8 apiece and given more opportunities (he bowled over 200 more overs than any previous season) he gained in confidence. Roy had always been a popular player with spectators and with his bowling being called upon more and more his popularity continued to increase. The Yorkshire crowds and indeed those in most counties were able to identify with him, share in his enjoyment of the game and all his own little ways which proved an endless source of entertainment to the spectators. This is how *The Field* described Kilner's behaviour when called upon to bowl:

'When he was put on to bowl each fieldsman knew where he had to go, but even while he was removing his sweater, Kilner would move two or three of them to different places. Another man or two would be shifted while he was taking his imaginary run to the wicket, and then when all was ready he would survey the field in the manner of a general watching the disposition of his troops. At the last moment he would move another man or two, and the first two overs seldom passed without more shifting. Yet so quickly were all these operations carried out that Kilner could never be accused of wasting a moment's time.'

1922

Continued winter pratice in the yard of the Halfway House helped Kilner to further his bowling education. His brother Norman, was quite adamant that it was Roy who gave the name of 'Chinaman' to that wristy variety of slow left-arm bowling. Roy practised it constantly in the nets.

Returning to the rigors of the Championship, Yorkshire and Kilner began the season in spectacular fashion. The first 5 matches were all won against not over-demanding opposition. Two wins over Northampton-

Kilner taking the field with his team-mate and bowling colleague George Macaulay. (Kind permission of Mrs M. Kilner.)

shire by 10 wickets and innings victories over Glamorgan and Worcestershire followed. Derbyshire were also beaten by the comfortable margin of 251 runs.

With the bat Kilner added to his tally of hundreds with 117 against Worcestershire and 124 against Northamptonshire yet again. Perhaps even more startling though, he took 21 wickets for 142 runs in those first five games.

Geoffrey Wilson was by now the Yorkshire skipper, a position he held for 3 seasons, seasons of great success for the club. After a draw with Leicestershire, Lancashire were beaten by 6 wickets at Sheffield. Lancashire made 307, Tyldesley, 178 and after Yorkshire failed by only one run to overtake that total, Lancashire collasped to 144 all out with Rhodes, four for 28 and Kilner, three for 25. Yorkshire then knocked off the required runs with Sutcliffe making 73 not out and Kilner again prominant with a quick 47.

Warwickshire were beaten by an innings and rain ruined the match at Bradford against Surrey. Winning ways returned with yet another innings victory this time Middlesex were the victims. Yorkshire's first defeat of the season came against Nottinghamshire. This time it was Yorkshire's turn to suffer an innings defeat.

That setback served merely to inspire Yorkshire to lift their game a further notch, the next 13 games brought 9 wins and 4 draws. Kilner played his part to the full. Against Sussex at Hull he took four for 19 and three for 13 in a match which Yorkshire won by an innings and 10 runs. Sussex managed only 95 and 20 all out in their completed innings. In the drawn game at Harrogate he picked up six Essex batsmen for 22 and ended with match figures of eleven for 51. In the top-of-the-table clash at Trent Bridge he bowled better than ever taking four for 15 in 18 overs as he and Robinson (five for 20) helped Yorkshire to a 5 wicket win.

Yorkshire's amazing run ended at Bradford in the match against Hampshire beaten by 5 wickets.

Kilner captured five for 38 from 37 overs at Lord's in the match with Middlesex which drifted to a draw. In the match with Surrey which also ended without any positive result he scored 89, out of a partnership of 173 with Sutcliffe.

At Bournemouth in the return with Hampshire, Yorkshire gained some revenge for their earlier defeat. Trailing on first innings by 21, Hampshire started their second innings with the match nicely balanced but were destroyed by Kilner who took six for 13 as Hampshire were shot out for 44 and Yorkshire completed a comfortable 10 wicket win. Kilner had a match analysis of ten for 90.

It had proved a close battle with Nottinghamshire but in the end Yorkshire were crowned Champions having won 19 of their 30 matches and lost only two. Roy Kilner had passed the 1,000 mark yet again with 1,198 runs at 27.22 which included not only two hundreds but 6 other scores of 50 or more. His bowling figures, though captured much attention. His seasons figures read:

Overs	Maidens	Runs	Wkts	Avge	5wI	10wM
1081.1	409	1797	122	14.72	6	2

The true test of any allrounder had been passed, Kilner having achieved the 'double' of 1,000 runs and 100 wickets for the first time in his career. His bowling feats against Essex and Hampshire were the highlights although he also enjoyed success for the North in the match against the South at Eastbourne where he took five for 11. His new-found consistency with the ball was the key to the success and it lifted him into the top flight of left arm slow bowlers in the country. For all the hours spent in the backyard of the Halfway House, Kilner was reaping the rewards.

1923

During the winter of 1922–3 Roy accepted a coaching engagement with H.H. The Maharajah of Patiala and journeyed to India where he participated in several matches alongside his county colleague, Wilfred Rhodes. Few records can be found of his cricketing exploits whilst in India but he did appear in three particular games which The Association of Cricket Statisticians now regard as being first class and the full scorecards of which can be found in their 'Guide to First Class Cricket Matches Played in India'. Some statisticians argue that these matches were of doubtful first-class status and should not be regarded as so. Whatever the arguments for and against their status, Kilner certainly enjoyed himself. Playing for the Europeans & Parsis against Hindus & Muslims in November 1922 he had scores of 14 and 34, bowled in the 2nd innings by Rhodes, he also took a wicket in each innings of that match. For all India (Europeans) against All India (Indians) in Bombay in early December he struck 128 and 49 not out as his side won by 7 wickets. In the Northern India Tournament in March 1923, Kilner had an outstanding match making 50 and 13 for the Europeans and then with the ball took six for 16 in the 1st innings and two for 7 in the 2nd (match figures of 8 for 23) as Hindus were beaten by 306 runs. His time in India kept him in good shape and by all accounts he thoroughly enjoyed the trip, so much so that he returned to the sub-continent the following winter.

There was very little time to readjust to the English weather before the 1923 season got underway with a visit to Cardiff to play Glamorgan. Kilner was immediately in the thick of things after Macaulay had destroyed Glamorgan in the first innings with seven for 13, Kilner went one better in the second with figures of eight for 26 as Yorkshire won by 9 wickets.

Worcestershire were shot out for 76 in their first innings, with Robinson, four for 41 and Kilner, three for 9, Yorkshire winners by an innings. At Bradford Middlesex went the same way, caught on a wet wicket they were bowled out for 122 and 60, Kilner the chief destroyer in the 2nd innings with six for 14, nine for 42 in the match from 40.4 overs. In the drawn match with Lancashire at Old Trafford, the Red Rose county batted for over 100 overs making 108 all out, Kilner five for 33. After just 4 matches he had 27 wickets to his name at a cost of only 157 runs in 138.3 overs.

He took on the role of allrounder in the next match against Worcestershire, top scoring in Yorkshire's total of 113 with 60 and had bowling figures of three for 30 and three for 8 to seal a Yorkshire win by 85 runs.

A rain affected draw with Kent at Sheffield was followed by another innings win this time at the expense of Derbyshire. Kilner producing impressive match figures of 8 for 69. Surely such outstanding form could not be maintained?

Nottinghamshire won a thrilling game at Headingley by 3 runs but that merely started Yorkshire on a run of 13 successive victories, one of the best of which came in the match with Surrey at Sheffield where Kilner's bowling reached new heights. Yorkshire batted first and thanks to sound tail-end batting made a respectable 278 all out. Surrey were dismissed for 224 with Kilner taking four for 78. Yorkshire fell away badly and were all out for 129 leaving their opponents only 184 to win and at 127 for two that seemed to be the way things would turn out. Robinson then took three quick wickets and Kilner applied the 'killer' touch after having dismissed Ducat earlier in the Surrey innings he took their last five wickets for only 15 runs in the following manner:

P. G. H. Fender	bowled Kilner	6
J. W. Hitch	caught Dolphin b. Kilner	0
H. A. Peach	bowled Kilner	0
H. Strudwick	bowled Kilner	0
R. F. Lowe	l.b.w. bowled Kilner	2

Roy finished with figures of six for 22 from 25.2 overs, ten for 100 in the match and Yorkshire had won a match which had seemed lost. Amazing to think that Kilner was under the impression that Surrey only needed 7 to win not 27 and his team mates recalled afterwards that he went white through the keenness and concentration of his bowling efforts.

He was called into the Players XI for the fixture in mid-July at Lord's where he bowled 26 overs in the Gentlemen's one and only innings. He was rewarded with three for 66. He made only 8 when the Players batted.

His batting during the season was never quite up to the standards he had set in previous years and for the first time since 1912 he failed to score a century during the entire summer but he made several important contributions with the willow and passed 50 on 9 occasions. One of those scores came against Essex where he made 72 in Yorkshire's 280 run victory.

If his batting went into temporary decline his bowling continued its upward trend. In the drawn match with Nottinghamshire he took six for 42 from 38 overs. At Leicester, Yorkshire won by an innings thanks to Rhodes, eight for 76 and Kilner, seven for 69, in the match. His dominance of Surrey continued in the return fixture at The Oval which was spoilt by rain. Surrey compiled 360, Kilner five for 93, and Yorkshire were 88 for 2 when the end came.

The smiling cricketer turned in another allround performance of the highest class in the match at Portsmouth against Hampshire. Match figures of five for 12 and top score with 77 out of a Yorkshire total of 206.

Surrey were beaten by 7 wickets in the last Championship fixture of the season and Yorkshire were Champions for the 2nd year running with Nottinghamshire again having to settle for the runners-up position.

The Yorkshire team were a grim, determined lot, a machine-like force which rolled over any opposition if they were less than determined not to lose. Survival against Yorkshire was the paramount consideration of most sides in the Championship. Kilner, though, stood out from the ranks, the cheerful member of the side, the entertainer always keen to please the spectator with his play. That he certainly did in the summer of 1923. He made 1401 runs at 34.17, but his batting ability had never been in doubt, his bowling was a different matter entirely. He was not only the most accurate bowler for the County but the leading wicket-taker as well, 143 at 12 runs each. In all matches he took 158 wickets at 12.90 and was second in the national averages behind Wilfred Rhodes.

His allround efforts had earned him a Test Trial and appearances for the Players against the Gentlemen at Lord's and also in early September at Scarborough where he made 31 and 10 and took three for 34 in the Gentlemen's first innings.

Praise for Kilner's achievements, especially with the ball in 1923, was quick to follow and A. W. Pullin summed up the comments when describing Kilner's summer of success in his 'history' of the club:

Kilner spins the ball probably better than any slow bowler in England, and it must have been noted that he bowls over the wicket with a frequency very unusual in the case of left-arm bowlers. The effect is to

By 1923 Roy Kilner had become a genuine allround cricketer and a left-arm slow bowler of the highest class. (Courtesy of T. Woodhouse.)

make a contrast with Rhodes which unsettles the batsman, also it enables Kilner occasionally to slip in his fast "going away" ball by which many batsmen have been taken unawares, or get them leg-before-wicket with an illusive straight one.

The development of Roy Kilner as a bowler can be cited as a signal example of the joint virtues of adaptability and painstaking endeavour. When he was first introduced into county cricket it was as a left-handed batsman only that he was expected to excel. It was known he could bowl, but there were already three left-hand bowlers in the eleven in George Hirst, Wilfred Rhodes and Alonzo Drake. The retirement of Hirst on taking up coaching duties at Eton, and the death of Drake opened up a new situation, and it is to the special credit of Kilner that he qualified by practice and study to fill one of the places thus vacated. He has perfected his finger spin by assidous practice and the placing of the field to his bowling has received much greater study than some pavilion critics seem to imagine.'

R. W. Frank, Captain of Yorkshire 2nd XI between 1900 and 1914, writing in the same book puts Kilner's allround ability into prespective: 'Of one thing I do feel especially pleased, and that is that I always urged Roy Kilner to make himself into a bowler. He received all the tuition possible, and with his own perseverance he eventually succeeded, with the result that today he is one of the most useful members of the team and one of the best all-round players in England.'

His opportunity to prove that statement correct would be fully tested during the season of 1924.

TEST CRICKETER AND TOURIST

'ROY KILNER, who on the general form of 1923 seems clearly marked out for Test Match honours. . .'

That opening comment in the 1924 edition of *Wisden Cricketers' Almanack* who had selected him as one of their 'Five bowlers of the Year' was a prediction which was to become a reality during the season of 1924 with the visit to England of the South African tourists.

Kilner, meanwhile, had again occupied the winter months in India, coaching and playing a little. Such winter employment kept him in good shape and allowed him much more time to practice the weaker part of his allround game, his bowling.

Yorkshire's pre-season tour of Scotland was ruined by the weather but that mattered little when their Championship campaign got underway at Cardiff with an overwhelming win by an innings and 177 runs. Kilner was immediately amongst the wickets with nine for 42 in the match. He followed that with six for 41 against Gloucestershire in a match Yorkshire won easily by 8 wickets.

At Headingley Kilner and Oldroyd added 102 for the 5th wicket, Oldroyd going on to score 103, Kilner making 50.

On a wet wicket at Bradford, Yorkshire scraped home by 3 wickets in a closely contested game with Nottinghamshire, Kilner four for 28 in Nottinghamshire's 2nd innings total of 92 all out maintained his early season demolition of the opposition.

At Lord's Yorkshire were without Kilner, Macaulay, Holmes and Sutcliffe who were all involved in the Test Trial and that allowed Middlesex to beat them by an innings and 152 runs.

The match against the South African tourists at Sheffield ended in a draw although Kilner took four for 30 in South Africa's first innings.

The Roses game with Lancashire at Leeds was a remarkable affair. Lancashire batted for over 90 overs in compiling 113, Macaulay six for 40 and Kilner two for 28 in 26.2 overs. Oldroyd with 37 and Kilner, 35, put

Yorkshire in a reasonable position at 115 for 5 but they fell away badly to 130 all out. Lancashire faired even worse and were dismissed for 74, Macaulay and Kilner, four wickets apiece. Requiring only 58 to win, Yorkshire never recovered from being 3 for three and were bowled out for only 33. Dick Tydlesley taking six for 18, Kilner though always one to relish a fight battled to the end and was not out on 13. Any Yorkshire versus Lancashire match brought out the best in Roy Kilner and his comments to Neville Cardus during one of their 'many talks' summed up his feelings on the matter:
'Ay', it's a reight match, Lancasheer and Yorksheer. Tha knows, t'two teams turn up on Bank Holiday, and we meets in t'dressin room, and we all says "Good mornin'!" to one another. And then we never speaks agean for three days!'

For the 1st Test Match of the summer at Edgbaston against South Africa, England selected five new caps amongst them were two Yorkshire players, Herbert Sutcliffe to open the batting with Jack Hobbs and the other was Roy Kilner who's early season form particularly with the ball had made him very difficult to ignore.

Solid batting from England throughout allowed them to score 438 all out and although no one scored a century there were significant contributions from Hobbs 76, Sutcliffe 64, Woolley 64, Hendren 74 and Kilner batting at number 7 in the order made 59 before being caught and bowled by Pegler.

South Africa were shot out on the 2nd morning for 30 as Gilligan, six for 7 and Tate, four for 12, ran riot. They faired much better in their 2nd innings and with Caterall making 120, South Africa were eventually bowled out for 390 but still lost by an innings and 18 runs. Gilligan and Tate again shared the wickets but Kilner was given 22 overs of which ten were maidens, nought for 40 his final figures. It had been a pleasing if not outstanding 1st Test. A little surprisingly he was omitted from the England side at Lord's and Headingley but was recalled for the 4th Test at Old Trafford where rain ended the game on the 1st day after South Africa had reached 116 for 4, Kilner bowled 12 overs, no wicket for 19.

Yorkshire marched on meantime, after their defeat at the hands of Lancashire their next 19 games produced nine draws and ten wins.

The highlight of Kilner's season came not in a match for Yorkshire but for the Players at Lord's in July. They made 514 in their 1st innings with Hobbs 118. Runs came slowly until the last hour of the day when Kilner – 'played free and attractive cricket. . .'. On the 2nd morning he and Tate attacked the bowling, Kilner going on to make 113. The Gentlemen were all out for 130 thanks to 'Tich' Freeman with six for 52. By lunch on the final day the Gentlemen had reached 112 for 3 and the match looked likely to end as a draw. Kilner though had other ideas and in quick succession dismissed Foster, Lyon, Gilligan, White and Robertson-Glasgow. By 2.50 p.m. the match was over. In the Gents' 2nd innings Kilner had taken 6 wickets for 20 runs to add to his splendid hundred. He played also in the game at Scarborough in September but was less successful scoring 2 in his only innings and taking one for 25 from 16 overs.

On the bowling front in particular Kilner reaped a rich harvest during the season. In the game at The Oval he dismissed ten Surrey batsmen in the match at a cost of 153 runs but Yorkshire were outplayed and lost the game by 109 runs.

In the following match at Portsmouth, a match which Yorkshire desperately needed to win, Hampshire were bowled out for 74 and 97, Kilner had match figures of 11 for 48 from 48 overs.

Yorkshire still needed victory in their last fixture of the season to ensure them the title for the 3rd successive year. On a drying wicket at Hove, Sussex were bowled out for 60, thanks to Kilner, five for 18 and Rhodes, three for 10. Yorkshire made 253 for 9 declared and Sussex again fell victim to Kilner who this time finished with seven for 37, a match analysis of 12 for 55. With Middlesex and Surrey drawing their game, Yorkshire were crowned Champions.

Kilner's batting form for Yorkshire was generally poor during the 1924 season and that was reflected in his average, 537 runs at 17.90 with a highest score of only 50 from 33 innings played. His bowling thankfully made for far healthier reading, 134 wickets at 13.01 for Yorkshire and he finished in 2nd place in the national averages behind his team mate George Macaulay who had had a wonderful season, in all matches he took 190 wickets.

Kilner's Test chance had seemed lost after his limited success at Edgbaston having got little opportunity to make amends in the rain-ruined 4th Test. As an allrounder his general form had been moderate, but as a bowler alone it had again been a splendid summer. It was probably though still somewhat of a surprise when his name was announced in the M.C.C. party under A. E. R. Gilligan to tour Australia in the winter of 1924–5.

A century on his debut 'down under' must have given him great pleasure. That innings of 103 against Western Australia would remain his highest score on the tour. He produced good performances in two matches against less than testing opposition, 63 against Coldfields Association XV and seven for 36 in another non-first-class fixture at Toowoomba. He was however omitted from the England side for the first two Test Matches both of which Australia won.

Against Ballarat XV he took six for 27 and made 64 with the bat. He was given his chance in the 3rd Test at Adelaide. Australia made 489 thanks to Jack Ryder who scored 201 not out. Roy got through 56 eight-ball overs, 7 maidens and took four wickets for 127 runs. England had lost the services of Maurice Tate and their captain, Arthur Gilligan, through injury early in the Australian innings and later 'Tich' Freeman, was also forced to retire from the bowling attack with a bruised wrist. The loss of three front-line bowlers made Kilner's performance even more important and as Gilligan later commented when paying tribute to the Yorkshire left arm bowler: '. . .this was a truly great performance.'

England, thanks mainly to Hobbs and Hendren, came within 124 runs of the Australians but then overnight rain altered conditions so completely that Australia's last seven wickets fell for only 39 runs in an hour. Roy took four of them from 22.1 overs costing 51 runs. It gave England the slightest hope, but despite their consistent batting they fell tantalisingly short of their target by 11 runs and so Australia went 3–nil up in the series. Kilner had batted to the end and made 24 batting at number seven.

He enjoyed himself against Tasmania with five for 35 and went one better against Victoria with 5 wickets in each innings, ten for 66 in the match.

England gained some revenge for their defeat at Adelaide with an innings victory at Melbourne. After making 548 with Sutcliffe scoring his fourth century of the series, Kilner contributed his highest Test score of 74. Australia were dismissed for 269 and 250, Kilner playing his part to the full with three for 29 and two for 41 in the match.

Australia were back to their best in the 5th and final Test winning by 307 runs. In Australia's 1st innings 295, Kilner took four for 97 from 38 overs and in England's 167 he made 25 but failed to take any wickets in Australia's 2nd innings which left England needing 454 to win. They collapsed against Charlie Grimmett, six for 37 and were all out for 146, Kilner made one.

The tour averages were headed by Herbert Sutcliffe, what a trip it had been for the Yorkshire opener. Kilner also had a good tour, although his bowling proved more impressive than his batting overall. He scored 448 runs on the trip from 19 innings at an average of 24.88, his highest score being the century he scored in the opening fixture.

His best bowling came against New South Wales where he took six for 145 and he finished the tour with 40 wickets at 25.17.

The season of 1925 was a very special one for Roy Kilner. The Yorkshire authorities had seen fit to grant him a benefit for his loyal years of service to the club. Certainly there could not have been a more popular choice, not only in Yorkshire but throughout the country. He was loved and respected wherever he went.

It was again a highly successful summer for both Yorkshire and Roy. Although a new captain was at the helm, Major A. Lupton aged 46 having replaced G. Wilson, the end result was exactly the same, Yorkshire were

The 1924–5 M.C.C. team which toured Australia:
Standing: H. Howell, R. K. Tyldesley, A. P. F. Chapman, F. C. Toone *(manager)*, M. W. Tate, W. W. Whysall, J. L. Bryan.
Seated: F. E. Woolley, J. W. Hearne, J. W. H. T. Douglas, A. E. R. Gilligan *(captain)*, J. B. Hobbs, E. H. Hendren, H. Strudwick.
Front: R. Kilner, A. P. Freeman, H. Sutcliffe, A. Sandham.
It was not a successful trip, they lost four Tests although they did win the 4th Test at Melbourne by an innings. Kilner enjoyed a successful tour with bat and ball. (From Pageant of Cricket *by David Frith.)*

County Champions for the fourth year running, golden years indeed. Surrey were runners-up and Lancashire finished third.

With no Test Matches to distract Kilner he recovered his best county form and reached the 'double' for the 3rd time in his career. His batting pleasingly was back at its best and hundreds came against Warwickshire (124) and M.C.C. (100 not out). His final run tally of 1068 at an average of 30.51 also included 7 other scores of 50 or more.

He continued to spin out the opposition but on plumb wickets he tended to resort to bowling leg-theory using the seam. It was a tactic he tended to over-do in the last few seasons of his career and certainly the leading cricket journals of the period including *The Cricketer* tended to criticise him in this respect. As his bowling figures tended to reflect in the last three summers of his life, that criticism was probably justified.

The highlights of 1925, from a bowling point of view, came at Bristol where he took four for 10 against Gloucestershire, at Hull against Leicestershire, he took three wickets in four balls. Remarkably he also had innings figures of five for 14 on two occasions, one at Bradford in the match with Sussex and the other against the 'old enemy', Lancashire at Bramhall Lane. In total he took 131 wickets at 17.92 each.

Neville Cardus, that great writer of cricket prose asked Kilner about the general state of the game, the perfect pitches, the high scoring in Australia, the slow batting and poor bowling. His answer was typical and bluntly honest yet as always humourous:
'T' game's all reight. It's crowd that's wrong – it wants educating up t'game. Listen to me – when I were a young lad I goes up to London and there I sees a play by Shakespeare. And by gum, it did make me tired and weary wi' yawning. When I gets home I says to mi father, "No more Shakespeare for me!" But mi father, he says, "Now look ere, Roy, lad; tha's just talking folly. Shakespeare's good enough for me, and 'e's good enough for thee. Tha wants educating up to him, thats what tha wants." And it's same wi t'crowd and county cricket. They wants educatin' up to it!'

There was no more recognisable cricketer playing the game in 1925 than Roy Kilner, with his cap askew and smiling round face he was popular with his fellow team-mates and spectators alike. Friendly and warm with everyone he encountered, it could truly be said he had no enemies, he was far too likeable a man for that. His benefit match against Middlesex at Headingley underlined his popularity and proved a great financial success. Holmes was delayed on the train travelling to the game and so Maurice Leyland was sent in to open the batting with Sutcliffe and they set about adding 218 for the 1st wicket. Holmes came in at number 4, he and Sutcliffe, who eventually made 235, added 135 together as Yorkshire declared at 528 for 6. Rain helped Middlesex save the game after they had been dismissed in their first innings for 184.

The M.C.C. party which toured the Caribbean in 1925–26. This picture was taken in Port of Spain in February 1926 on the occasion of Lord Harris's 75th birthday. For Kilner it was a disappointing venture. (From Pageant of Cricket *by David Frith.)*

Kilner's final benefit figure was £4,106 which beat the previous highest benefit in 1904 by George Herbert Hirst. It merely reflected the warmth of feeling which existed for the laughing cricketer.

M.C.C. had promised to send out a tour party to the West Indies and the trip was eventually organised for the winter of 1925–6. The side was led by F. S. Gough-Calthorpe of Warwickshire (the original captain, R. St L. Fowler having died in June 1925), and included several familiar names: Hon L. H. Tennyson (Hampshire) amongst the amateur ranks and from the professionals: W. E. Astill (Leicestershire), W. R. Hammond (Gloucestershire), C. F. Root (Worcestershire), Tiger Smith (Warwickshire) and Holmes and Kilner of Yorkshire.

The tour opened in early January against a Colts team in which Kilner took seven for 24. It was a disappointing tour for Kilner overall, his highest score was only 54 made against Jamaica towards the end of the trip and with the ball, six for 83 against Trinidad and then seven for 50 in the 1st of three matches with Jamaica were the only bright spots. He averaged 22.63 with the bat and his 34 wickets cost 29.50 apiece. Overall it was a trip to forget quickly and concentrate instead on another 'double' for Yorkshire.

A ten-wicket win against Essex at Leyton got the season off to a successful start for Yorkshire and Kilner who took ten for 116 in the match. In the return fixture at Harrogate, Kilner picked up seven for 68 in the game to round-off a 'double' triumph against Essex.

In the Roses match at Bradford he was largely responsible for Yorkshire's innings victory. After hitting 85 including 2 sixes and 10 fours he helped dismiss Lancashire for 159 and 73 with figures of three for 40 and in the 2nd innings, four for 19.

Kilner's 17th and final first class century came at Lord's. After Middlesex had been dismissed by Macaulay, Yorkshire ran up 415 with Kilner, although dropped four times, hitting a brilliant 150 sharing in a 5th wicket partnership with Rhodes of 108, of which the latter made just 27. Middlesex still managed to escape with a creditable draw thanks to Patsy Hendren with 213.

The Ashes series of 1926 began with a rain-ruined match at Trent Bridge, Kilner having been selected in the eleven got no opportunity with either bat or ball as the weather allowed only 50 minutes play on the first day, no play was possible on the 2nd or 3rd days.

In the 2nd Test at Lord's, Australia batted first making 383 due largely to Bardsley who hit 193, Kilner bowled 34.5 overs, 11 maidens and took four for 70. He was not called upon to bat as England with hundreds from Hobbs and Hendren made 475 for 3 declared. Australia held out for a draw on 194 for 5.

On his home territory at Headingley in the 3rd Test, Kilner toiled away

The Yorkshire side under A. W. Lupton (circa 1925–27). Still a major force in the cricket world but dethroned as County Champions in 1926 by rivals Lancashire for the first time since 1921. (Courtesy of Tony Woodhouse.)

through 37 overs costing 106 runs and took the wickets of T. J. E. Andrews and Gregory as Australia made 494 all out. England batted inconsistently, Kilner being third top-scorer with 36 out of 294 all out. Following on they batted far better and finished on 254 for 3, Hobbs and Sutcliffe again provided the back-bone of the English batting with an opening partnership of 156.

His final appearance for the Players against the Gentlemen came in the match after the 3rd Test. In an innings of 72 which lasted only 80 minutes he hit 10 fours but had very little success when the Gentlemen batted getting through 37 overs costing 118 runs without picking up a wicket. It was a different story in the following game at Bradford against Middlesex. Having helped Yorkshire to a 76-run lead on first innings with 44, he then bowled at his best as Middlesex at one stage 51 for 2 collapsed and allowed Yorkshire to win with ease by 10 wickets. Kilner had taken eight for 40 in Middlesex's 2nd innings and ten for 117 in the match.

The 4th Test Match at Old Trafford towards the end of July sadly was Kilner's last of the series and of his career. In yet another drawn match, Australia made 335 in their 1st innings, Kilner's one and only wicket being that of Ponsford whom he caught and bowled for 23. England managed 305 for 5, Kilner remaining 9 not out in his final Test innings before the match again ended in stalemate. Kilner did not hold his place for the final Test which saw a triumphant victory for England led by Percy Chapman.

Lancashire won the County Championship by a short margin, their percentage being 75.71 to Yorkshire's 74.28. It brought to an end Yorkshire's golden run of Championship victories. Test calls robbed Yorkshire, at various stages of the summer of the services of Sutcliffe, Rhodes, Kilner and Macaulay. Six players scored 1,000 runs for the season including Kilner who had 1187 runs to his name at 37.09. He took 96 wickets for Yorkshire but in all matches took 107 at 22.52 each. He had his effective days and as always he had been consistent but his general level of performance showed signs to some extent of deterioration, although his skill and experience had still allowed him to achieve the 'double' for the 4th time in his career and at the age of 35, he still had several years of good cricket in him, no one doubted that for a moment.

'A YORKSHIRE WICKET HAS FALLEN. . .'

The M.C.C. tour party which visited India during the winter of 1926–7 was without the services of several leading players including Hobbs, Sutcliffe, Woolley and Roy Kilner who had all declined the M.C.C.'s invitation for their individual reasons. Roy preferred to stay at home with his wife and growing boys and instead tried his hand at learning to drive a motor car, the allrounder indeed!

The English summer of 1927 was something of a let down not only for Yorkshire C.C.C. but also for Roy Kilner. The county slipped to 3rd place in the Championship, a relative failure after the glory years between 1922 and 1925 whilst Kilner failed to take a 100 wickets in the season for the first time in 6 years, his 86 wickets were taken at 23.68 each. On the batting front he passed 1,000 runs by only 4 at 33.46 and he failed to score a century. He made six scores of 50 or more, his best being 90 not out against Gloucestershire and 91 not out in the final match of the season against Sussex. That match at Hove, although he didn't know it at the time was his swan-song from Championship cricket, he could not have asked for a finer finale. Sussex were dismissed for 221 with Macaulay taking five for 83 and Yorkshire replied with 302, Kilner top scoring with his innings of 91 not out which gave his side a 1st innings lead of 81. Sussex could muster only 120 in their 2nd innings as Kilner completed a fine allround performance by taking five for 21 from 21.1 overs, eight for 66 in the match.

Kilner's final first class match and the last game of the 1927 season was at Scarborough against the M.C.C. He hit 43 in the 1st innings and followed it with a bright unbeaten 51 in the 2nd innings as Yorkshire won by 8 wickets. Unbeknown to anyone the career of one of the game's most lovable character's was at an end.

Leaving the disappointments of the summer behind him, Roy received an invitation from H.H. The Maharajah of Patiala to tour India during the winter of 1927–8 and coach at the Rajendra Club in Punjab. From the very first day that invitation was received there seemed to be a shadow over

Probably one of the last photographs ever taken of Roy during that fateful trip to India in 1927–28. (By kind permission of Mrs M. Kilner.)

Kilner, his sister, Mollie, later commented that Roy was reluctant to accept almost as though he had a premonition that something would go wrong. He and his wife were also having a house built at Sandal near Wakefield which made his decision even harder.

Eventually after much thought he decided to accept the invitation, tragedy struck almost immediately. Irving Washington had never been in the greatest of health since being forced to give up the game through illness in 1902. He had continued to play with Mitchell Main up until the outbreak of World War One and for many years afterwards he was President of the Mexborough & District Cricket League. He was the sanitory inspector for the Wombwell U.D. Council for 16 years before becoming a coal agent for Mitchell Main Colliery just before the final illness which ended his life at his home, The Limes, Barnsley Road, Wombwell on October 20th 1927 aged 47. There had been no greater supporter and inspiration to the young Roy Kilner than Irving Washington, now Roy had to bid an affectionate farewell to his beloved Uncle Irving before embarking for Africa the day before his uncle's untimely death. It must have been a sad farewell.

His visit to India unde the shadow of his uncle's death would have put strain on even the most cheerful of men, Kilner was no exception. His actions on that trip all suggest he was weighed down with pessimism and strong feelings of melancholy. He recorded all his scores whilst in India on his bat with a view to presenting it to his oldest son, Roy junior, upon his return to England, this was something he had never before been known to do. His record was impressive and that bat he used on that trip still bears the scores to prove it. Against Rajendra he made 283 not out for Rajendra Gymkhana in Delhi in November of 1927, an innings which included 40 fours. His other innings were 90, 70, 47, 48 and 90, all not out. Another indication of his depressive state came in a letter to Abe Waddington, his county colleague back in Yorkshire. In the letter all the little reminiscences of the Yorkshiremen were referred to in a past tense almost as if he did not expect to play for them again.

Where and exactly how he contracted the germ which would later end his life is unkown, even today it remains a mystery. Several theories have been suggested, one by Arthur Dolphin and Maurice Leyland, who were both with him in India, they recalled Roy eating oysters which they themselves declined. The illness developed over a fortnight before Roy's arrival back on English soil while he was travelling overland from Marseilles. He had tried to shake off the feeling by perspirations but later the shivering attacks returned.

By the time he reached Southampton on the boat it was obvious the illness had taken a strong hold and he was put immediately to bed. He had accepted an engagement to give a display of cricket at Messrs Gamage's in

The emotional scenes outside Wombwell Parish Church on Tuesday 10th April 1928. Conservative estimates put the number of people who attended Kilner's funeral that day at 100,000, the figure may truly have been closer to 150,000. Each one came to say farewell to their hero. (By kind permission of Mrs Taylor.)

High Holborn, London but that was cancelled and instead he was conveyed from London in a motor-ambulance straight back to his home in Wombwell. He had asked his wife to meet him upon his arrival at Southampton and that fact added to his refusal to have treatment in the South underlined how sick he really was. It seemed his dearest wish was to return to his home town, almost as if he could feel death near and so wanted to be with his family in his beloved Yorkshire before the end came.

On Tuesday 27th March, Roy arrived back in Wombwell and he was driven straight to his doctor, Dr W.C. Jardine, who examined him in the ambulance. He was taken to his home in Barnsley Road but his worsening condition required further attention and shortly afterwards he was transferred to Kendray Fever Hospital near Barnsley. Mrs Elizabeth Hanby recalls how despite his illness he was cheerful still. As he was being carried to the ambulance he spoke briefly to her:

'I won't be long as I'm back and we will have that drive round Bashers (Bashforths) Lane. I can drive with one arm now!'

Such a strong and determined man as Kilner would surely pull through this illness which by now had been diagnosed as a form of enteric fever. He had always loved a battle and this was by far the greatest battle he had ever faced. The people of Wombwell were with him as always, hoping against hope that their hero would recover. Many people thought he had passed through the most critical moments of the illness. His wife spent many hours by his side and his family were also constantly with him.

The first few days of April saw Kilner's condition deteriorate as he became critical. On the evening of Thursday, 5th April 1928 his wife and parents were once again at his bedside. Just before 11 o'clock his parents left but his wife stayed on. At around 11.20 p.m. Roy Kilner, at the age of only 37, passed away, he was conscious to the end which was peaceful, the laughing cricketer of Wombwell was dead.

The following day, Friday 6th April, was Good Friday and so a general holiday yet the news of Roy's death spread quickly through Wombwell, passed on in hushed tones from mouth to mouth. All day there were callers, bringing regrets at the hotel, home of Seth Kilner. Drawn blinds and flags at half-mast expressed the town's grief and the Wombwell football players wore black rosettes. Mr John Belshaw, Chairman of the Wombwell Urban Council, summed up the whole town's feelings:

'The town has lost one of its greatest citizens. Of all of our sons, none has been more highly esteemed than Roy Kilner. We know that wherever he went he brought credit to his country, his county and the little colliery town from which he came. His success never spoiled him. In the name of the town of Wombwell, I should like to express our deep sense of loss at his death. Long live the spirit of Roy Kilner.'

Tributes and memories of Roy flooded in from all over the world, kind

Their faces tell it all; Wilfred Rhodes (far left), Abe Waddington (front centre) and George Hirst (far right) mourn the loss of a much loved colleague. (By kind permission of Mrs Taylor.)

words in every one, warm and glowing with affection for a man who's death was described by Neville Cardus thus:
'. . .it is like being told that some genial Yorkshire breeze has died and will never again blow over the faces of men and refresh them.'

Roy's funeral took place on Tuesday 10th April, it was always going to be an emotional occasion but surely few expected the scenes on that sad spring day. The spectacle was one of the most memorable that has ever taken place in Wombwell. It was a demonstration of pure affection unmatched probably before or since. Long before the time set for the cortege to set off, crowds of people began to line the streets of Wombwell. They came from all parts, many thousands walked from nearby towns and villages, from Rawmarsh, Swinton, Barnsley and Mexborough. Tram-cars and hundreds of private cars brought countless more into the little town. In fact there was considerable difficulty in maintaining a passage for normal traffic. The general business of the township was virtually totally suspended. The streets rapidly became packed as the appointed hour drew near, Wombwell seemed one dense mass of people. Conservative estimates suggest that over 100,000 people were present in the streets of Wombwell that day but in reality the figure may have been nearer 150,000.

All the previous day and that morning wreaths had been gathering at the Halfway House, these were placed in an upstairs room which was a sweet-smelling place with wreaths of red and white roses, narcissi, tulips and orchids. Two large vehicles were required to carry the wreaths which constituted a beautiful tribute when the cortege finally set off from the Halfway House.

The procession was led by the Wombwell Town Band, followed by the local corps of the St John Ambulance Association and the Wombwell Church Lads Brigade. On each side of the hearse walked his Yorkshire colleagues and behind it, Kilner's wife, a pathetic figure as she held the arm of her young son, Roy aged 12. All along the route from the Hotel to the church men and women stood quietly and reverently, blinds were drawn at practically every house and shop.

There was no room to move inside Wombwell Parish Church where Roy had worshipped, where he had been baptised and as a boy attended Sunday School. The Rector Sydney T. G. Smith opened his memoriam with these lines:
'A Yorkshire wicket has fallen, and one of Yorkshire's best men is out; and we lament his loss; not merely because it is the loss of a great cricketer, but because it is the loss of such a Cricketer as Roy Kilner was.'

At the cemetary there was probably a thousand or more people present for the actual interment. As a final tribute, Roy's Yorkshire colleagues acted as bearers. At one side walked George Hirst along with Rhodes, Sutcliffe, Holmes, Dolphin and Denton and on the other Leyland,

Roy's grave in Wombwell cemetary. One hundred years after his birth he is remembered still in the small mining town, the laughing cricketer of Wombwell lives on in the hearts of many.

Mitchell, Oldroyd, Robinson and Douglas, Abe Waddington was also present. Whilst relatives and intimate friends gathered round the open grave, Roy's colleagues stood a little distance away, waiting to offer their final greeting and farewell to their old friend. Quietly they walked up to the grave, and left it sadly and in tears.

And so it was all over, the remains of Roy Kilner were laid to rest, the massive crowd slowly dispersed and time moved on.

Roy Kilner lived a rich and full life cut down in his prime, perhaps his best days with Yorkshire were behind him, perhaps he was no longer one of the oustanding allrounders in England or a cricketer of Test class but that such a man as he should die so young was sorrowful indeed. He was loved and admired throughout the world, wherever he ventured he was popular for the way he played the game but perhaps more so for his friendly and warm approach. From Sydney to Bombay, in England and throughout the length and breath of Yorkshire he was loved but nowhere more so than in his home town of Wombwell. Today, a 100 years after his birth, he is remembered still for in Wombwell Roy Kilner's memory lives on, it probably always will.

'In Kilner, whom we've lost,
A figure taken from the field,
We shall not soon forget,
With everybody, rich and poor
A plucky unspoilt pet,
Hope of the present, future, past,
High on the rolls of fame,
A stalwart, holding firm and fast,
The honours of the game.'

THE LEGACY OF ROY KILNER

Two years after Roy Kilner's sad demise the 1930 Australian touring side came to Wombwell to pay their own tribute. Roy had made many friends 'Down Under' during his visit to the country with the 1924–5 M.C.C. party.

The spirit of Roy lived on in many households both in Wombwell and throughout the county, the number of children who were named Roy after their parents' hero is hard to estimate. It was the slightest of connections for many to the cheerful Yorkshire cricketer.

Roy's rise to national prominence through the ranks of Yorkshire cricket and eventually Test cricket brought his birthplace of Wombwell to an equal prominence it had not seen before. The Rector of Wombwell Parish Church, Rev Canon Sydney Smith who conducted the service at Roy's funeral summed it up perfectly:

'To be associated with him in any way was a privilege. Oneself as his Rector has shared in this pride, when perchance, far away from home and where the name "Wombwell" sounded remote to the people, there has nevertheless been a hesitancy to dismiss the name at its utterance, right off, as not being on the map; and then there has dawned an inspiration, and these far-off friends have slowly exclaimed "Why! Wombwell? Isn't that where Roy Kilner, the great Cricketer comes from?'

Seth Kilner (Roy's father) passed away on 7th October 1933 aged 68, having lost Roy in 1928, Margaret (Peggy) Kilner, their third daughter died on 20th November 1930 in her twenties. Roy's mum, Mary Alice lived on until the age of 79, she died on 16th April 1948. Strangely and if by fate, Roy's wife, Annie, was 68 years of age when she died on 5th April (the same date Roy passed away) 1959.

What became of Roy's two sons? Neither followed in their father's footsteps although Major was a difficult batsman to remove in local cricket and Roy junior played for Mitchell Main and Barnsley but never quite fulfilled his potential. Both took up military careers, Roy junior won the

Military Cross in the Second World War. Sadly both are now dead, a further link severed.

Roy's younger brother, Norman who forged a successful career with Warwickshire during the twenties and thirties became a first-class umpire following his retirement at the end of the 1937 season. After serving in the war he again turned to umpiring but in 1946 he was appointed head groundsman and coach at Birmingham University, a position he retired from in 1965. He died on 28th April 1979 aged 83.

In 1962 the local council named a new road in Wombwell – 'Roy Kilner Road' – as a permanent tribute to one of the town's most famous sons. The glory days of Mitchell Main though were long since over. When the Coal Board took over the old ground they provided a new venue close to Roy Kilner Road but as Norman Kilner later commented, times had changed: 'Unfortunately the colliers for whom it was intended never go near it – they are all on the golf course. We never dreamed of, nor even saw a Golf Club, it was all Cricket and Soccer.'

In 1951 the then Rector of Wombwell, the Rev George Needham gathered together a small group of cricket lovers to talk about the game and from that humble first meeting, the now famous Wombwell Cricket Lovers Society was formed. The Society's greatly admired coaching scheme has, over the years, battled hard to produce cricketers capable of following Kilner into the Yorkshire first team. The writer would like to think that its success in achieving that aim would have been greatly supported by Roy Kilner.

As a new decade dawns, hopes for the future naturally occupy most people's thoughts and who knows perhaps somewhere in this great county there is a small boy practising in a backyard with a broad smile on his face waiting to grace the game in the same way as the laughing cricketer of Wombwell once did.

MICK POPE
Piccadilly, Yorkshire
February 1990

BIBLIOGRAPHY

1. COLLECTIONS OF SCORES, ANNUALS AND REFERENCE WORKS

Bailey, Philip, Thorn, Philip and Wynne-Thomas, Peter, *Who's Who of Cricketers* (Feltham: Newnes Books, 1984)

Frindall, Bill, *The Wisden Book of Test Cricket 1877-1984* (London: Guild Publishing, 1985)

Frindall, Bill, *England Test Cricketers* (Collins Willow, 1989)

The Association of Cricket Statisticians, *Yorkshire Cricketers 1863-1985*, compiled and published by The Association of Cricket Statisticians

A Guide to First Class Cricket Matches played in India, compiled and published by the Association of Cricket Statisticians

John Wisden's Cricketers' Almanack (various years)

The Yorkshire C.C.C. year book (various years)

2. NEWSPAPERS

The Barnsley Chronicle
The Barnsley Independent
The Daily Express
The Field, the Country Gentleman's Newspaper
The Harrogate Herald
The Leeds Mercury
The Manchester Guardian
The Rotherham Advertiser
The Sheffield Daily Telegraph
The South Yorkshire Times
The Yorkshire Evening Post
The Yorkshire Post

3. JOURNALS & PERIODICALS

The Cricket Statistician
The Cricketer
Playfair Cricket Monthly

4. BOOKS

Farnsworth, Keith, *Before and After Bramhall Lane* (private publication, 1988)

Frith, David, *Pageant of Cricket* (MacMillan, London Ltd, 1987)

Greaves, George L., *Over the Summers Again* (Harrogate: The Club, 1976)

Green, Benny, *The Wisden Book of Cricket Obituaries* (Queen Anne Press, Macdonald & Co (Publishers) Ltd, 1986)

Hodgson, Derek, *The Official History of Yorkshire County Cricket Club* (Crowood Press, 1989)
Kilburn, J. M., *History of Yorkshire County Cricket 1924-1949* (Yorkshire C.C.C., 1950)
Pullin, A. W., *History of Yorkshire County Cricket 1903-1923* (Chorley & Pickersgill, 1924)
Roberts, E. L., *Yorkshire's 22 Championships 1893-1946* (Edward Arnold & Co, 1949)
Thomas, Peter, *Yorkshire Cricketers 1839-1939* (Hodgson, 1973)
Thomson, A. A., *Hirst and Rhodes* (Epworth, 1959)
Warner, Sir Pelham, *Gentlemen v. Players 1806-1949* (George G. Harrop & Co Ltd, 1950)
Woodhouse, A, *The History of Yorkshire C.C.C,* (Christopher Helm, 1989)
Woodhouse, A, Wilkinson, R. D. and Sokell, J. *Cricketers of Wombwell* (Wombwell Cricket Lovers' Society, 1965)
Wynne-Thomas, Peter, *The Complete History of Cricket Tours at Home and Abroad* (Guild Publishing, 1989)
Wynne-Thomas, Peter, *The Hamlyn A-Z of Cricket Records* (Hamlyn Publishing, 1983)

STATISTICS

by

ROY D. WILKINSON

STATISTICS: FOOTNOTE

The career figures quoted do not include 3 matches Kilner participated in during his visit to India in 1922–3 which are now considered first-class by The Association of Cricket Statisticians. The full scorecards of the three matches involved can be found in the A.C.S.'s Guide to First-Class Cricket Matches Played in India under the following page references:

Europeans & Parsis v Hindus & Muslims at Gymkhana Ground, Bombay, November 27, 28 and 29, 1922 – page 102

All India (Indians) v All India (Europeans) at Gymkhana Ground, Bombay, November 30, December 1 and 2, 1922 – page 103

Europeans v Hindus at Lawrence Gardens, Lahore, March 2, 3 and 4, 1923 – page 196

For the record Roy Kilner produced the following figures in the 3 games mentioned above:

Matches	Innings	N.O.	Runs	H.S.	Avge	100's	50's
3	6	1	288	128	57.60	1	1

Overs	Maidens	Runs	Wkts	Avge	5wI	10wM
81	22	195	12	16.25	1	–

ROY KILNER IN FIRST-CLASS CRICKET 1911-1927

COMPILED BY ROY D. WILKINSON

Born: Low Valley, Wombwell 17th October 1890
Died: Kendray, Barnsley 5th April 1928

Left-hand batsman: slow left-arm bowler

Debut for Yorkshire: v Somerset at Taunton, 18th May 1911
Last match for Yorkshire: v MCC at Scarborough, 31st August 1927

Debut for England: v South Africa at Birmingham, 14th June 1924
Last match for England: v Australia at Manchester, 24th July 1926

FIRST-CLASS MATCHES

BATTING AND FIELDING

Season	M	I	No	Runs	HS	Avge	100s	50s	Cent. P'Ships	c
1911	7	10	1	60	18	6.66	–	–	–	1
1912	23	30	5	570	83*	22.80	–	3	1	13
1913	30	50	4	1586	104	34.47	1	12	6	22
1914	29	44	1	1329	169	30.90	1	11	8	18
1919	32	43	4	1135	120	29.10	3	6	5	24
1920	29	38	2	1316	206*	36.55	3	5	7	19
1921	30	41	0	1137	166	27.73	2	5	3	25
1922	36	48	4	1198	124	27.22	2	6	5	24
1923	36	49	8	1401	79	34.17	–	9	6	26
1924	34	38	3	731	113	20.88	1	2	1	21
1924-25	12	19	1	448	103	24.88	1	2	2	5
1925	37	39	4	1068	124	30.51	2	7	3	15
1925-26	12	15	4	249	54	22.63	–	1	–	17
1926	35	35	3	1187	150	37.09	1	6	2	25
1927	31	41	11	1004	91*	33.46	–	6	1	10
Totals	413	540	55	14419	206*	29.72	17	81	50	265

OVERSEAS TOURS

1924-25 MCC to Australia
1925-26 MCC to West Indies

FIRST-CLASS MATCHES

BOWLING

Season	Overs	Mdns	Runs	Wkts	Avge	5 wkts in Inns	10 wkts in Match	Best in Inns
1911		Did	Not Bowl					
1912	167.3	58	338	16	21.12	–	–	4:66
1913	204.4	53	454	18	25.22	–	–	3:8
1914	84	15	305	1	305.00	–	–	1:59
1919	377.3	124	824	45	18.31	–	–	4:12
1920	359.2	124	684	27	25.33	–	–	4:10
1921	589.1	204	1147	61	18.80	2	–	5:29
1922	1081.1	409	1797	122	14.72	6	2	6:13
1923	1261.5	507	2039	158	12.90	7	2	8:26
1924	1159.4	479	1927	145	13.28	11	3	7:37
1924–25	†375.1	61	1007	40	25.17	4	1	6:145
1925	1229.2	465	2348	131	17.92	5	–	6:92
1925–26	424.5	128	1003	34	29.50	2	–	7:50
1926	1199.5	380	2410	107	22.52	5	2	8:40
1927	1049.5	353	2037	86	23.68	5	–	5:21
Totals	†375.1 9188.4	3360	18320	991	18.48	47	10	8:26

† 8–ball overs

FIRST-CLASS MATCHES FOR YORKSHIRE

BATTING AND FIELDING

Season	M	I	No	Runs	HS	Avge	100s	50s	Cent. P'Ships	c
1911	7	10	1	60	18	6.66	–	–	–	1
1912	23	30	5	570	83*	22.80	–	3	1	13
1913	30	50	4	1586	104	34.47	1	12	6	22
1914	29	44	1	1329	169	30.90	1	11	8	18
1919	31	42	4	1135	120	29.86	3	6	5	24
1920	28	36	2	1240	206*	36.44	3	5	7	19
1921	30	41	0	1137	166	27.73	2	5	3	25
1922	33	43	3	1132	124	28.30	2	6	5	24
1923	31	41	7	1265	79	37.20	–	9	6	21
1924	29	33	3	537	50	17.90	–	1	1	19
1925	35	37	4	1002	124	30.36	2	6	3	13
1926	28	30	1	1021	150	35.20	1	5	2	22
1927	31	41	11	1004	91*	33.46	–	6	1	10
Totals	365	478	46	13018	206*	30.13	15	75	48	231

BOWLING

Season	Overs	Mdns	Runs	Wkts	Avge	5 wkts in Inns	10 wkts in Match	Best in Inns
1911		Did	Not Bowl					
1912	167.3	58	338	16	21.12	–	–	4:66
1913	204.4	53	454	18	25.22	–	–	3:8
1914	84	15	305	1	305.00	–	–	1:59
1919	350.3	117	766	45	17.02	–	–	4:12
1920	353.2	122	667	27	24.70	–	–	4:10
1921	589.1	204	1147	61	18.80	2	–	5:29
1922	1005.1	383	1640	107	15.32	5	2	6:13
1923	1124.3	465	1715	143	11.99	7	2	8:26
1924	1046	432	1744	134	13.01	10	3	7:37
1925	1161.2	441	2182	123	17.73	5	–	6:92
1926	963	317	1859	96	19.36	5	2	8:40
1927	1049.5	353	2037	86	23.68	5	–	5:21
Totals	8099	2960	14854	857	17.33	39	9	8:26

COUNTY CHAMPIONSHIP MATCHES

BATTING AND FIELDING

Season	M	I	No	Runs	HS	Avge	100s	50s	Cent. P'Ships	c
1911	7	10	1	60	18	6.66	–	–	–	1
1912	19	24	5	489	83*	25.73	–	2	1	11
1913	26	43	3	1307	104	32.67	1	9	4	17
1914	26	41	1	1232	167	30.80	1	10	8	17
1919	26	34	4	955	115*	31.83	2	6	3	22
1920	26	33	2	1184	206*	38.19	3	4	7	18
1921	26	34	0	1060	166	31.17	2	5	3	20
1922	30	38	2	1085	124	30.13	2	6	5	23
1923	29	38	6	1126	79	35.18	–	8	4	19
1924	24	26	3	435	50	18.91	–	1	1	18
1925	31	32	2	734	124	24.46	1	4	3	12
1926	25	27	1	943	150	36.26	1	5	2	21
1927	28	36	9	901	91*	33.37	–	5	1	8
Totals	323	416	39	11511	206*	30.53	13	65	42	207

BOWLING

Season	Overs	Mdns	Runs	Wkts	Avge	5 wkts in Inns	10 wkts in Match	Best in Inns
1911		Did	Not Bowl					
1912	139	52	252	13	19.38	–	–	4:66
1913	179	48	373	14	26.64	–	–	3:23
1914	76	11	293	1	293.00	–	–	1:59
1919	274.2	97	573	38	15.07	–	–	4:12
1920	335.2	119	598	27	22.14	–	–	4:10
1921	485.1	178	898	51	17.60	2	–	5:29
1922	916.1	354	1454	101	14.39	5	2	6:13
1923	1073.3	455	1585	139	11.33	7	2	8:26
1924	868	366	1370	113	12.12	10	3	7:37
1925	1037.2	404	1891	116	16.30	5	–	6:92
1926	899	304	1706	91	18.74	5	2	8:40
1927	940.5	314	1848	80	23.10	5	–	5:21
Totals	7223.4	2702	12841	784	16.37	39	9	8:26

TEST MATCHES

BATTING AND FIELDING

Season	M	I	No	Runs	HS	Avge	100s	50s	Cent. P'Ships	c
1924(v S.A)	2	1	0	59	59	59.00	–	1	–	1
1924-25(v A)	3	5	0	129	74	25.80	–	1	1	2
1926(v A)	4	2	1	45	36	45.00	–	–	–	3
Totals	9	8	1	233	74	33.28		2	1	6

BOWLING

Season	Overs	Mdns	Runs	Wkts	Avge	5 wkts in Inns	10 wkts in Match	Best in Inns
1924(v S.A.)	34	16	59	0	–	–	–	–
1924–25(v A)	†179.1	35	399	17	23.47	–	–	4:51
1926(v A)	121.5	31	276	7	39.42	–	–	4:70
Totals	†179.1 155.5	82	734	24	30.58	–	–	4:51

† 8-ball overs

OPPONENTS — COUNTY CHAMPIONSHIP

BATTING AND FIELDING

Opponents	M	I	No	Runs	HS	Avge	100s	50s	Cent. P'Ships	c
Derbyshire	19	20	2	815	206*	45.27	1	4	6	14
Essex	19	21	1	421	85	21.05	–	2	2	16
Glamorgan	9	8	1	200	52	28.37	–	1	–	4
Glos	21	26	4	903	169	41.04	3	3	5	8
Hampshire	22	28	2	668	85	25.69	–	5	–	13
Kent	21	27	1	639	79	24.57	–	5	3	7
Lancashire	23	35	2	728	93	22.06	–	3	–	20
Leics	21	25	1	671	104	26.84	1	3	2	7
Middlesex	22	32	3	1052	150	36.27	1	6	4	13
Northants	23	30	4	1183	166	45.50	3	6	5	21
Notts	22	34	2	875	137	27.34	1	5	4	19
Somerset	15	17	3	261	59	18.64	–	2	–	12
Surrey	23	31	0	572	89	18.45	–	3	3	12
Sussex	23	30	3	871	91*	32.25	–	7	3	13
Warwicks	23	33	6	1204	124	44.59	2	8	3	18
Worcs	17	19	4	448	117	29.86	1	2	2	10
Totals	323	416	39	11511	206*	30.53	13	65	42	207

BOWLING

Opponents	Overs	Mdns	Runs	Wkts	Avge	5 wkts in Inns	10 wkts in Match	Best in Inns
Derbyshire	379.3	162	533	47	11.34	1	–	5:32
Essex	422	170	720	49	14.69	3	2	6:22
Glamorgan	216.3	84	366	40	9.15	2	1	8:26
Glos	456.4	187	735	47	15.63	–	–	4:10
Hampshire	500.2	168	970	53	18.30	3	2	6:13
Kent	382.5	103	818	28	29.21	1	–	5:48
Lancashire	679.1	294	969	54	17.94	2	–	5:14
Leicestershire	458.4	196	704	37	19.02	2	–	5:56
Middlesex	621.5	204	1289	65	19.83	4	1	8:40
Northants	301.2	132	518	45	11.51	1	–	5:34
Notts	587	214	1048	59	17.76	3	–	6:42
Somerset	249.4	89	506	28	18.07	–	–	4:40
Surrey	596.1	195	1248	63	19.80	5	2	6:22
Sussex	525	184	945	70	13.50	5	1	7:37
Warwickshire	534.5	199	974	62	15.70	5	–	6:26
Worcs	312.1	121	498	37	13.45	2	–	5:48
Totals	7223.4	2702	12841	784	16.37	39	9	8:26

OTHER MATCHES FOR YORKSHIRE

BATTING AND FIELDING

Opponents	M	I	No	Runs	HS	Avge	100s	50s	Cent. P'Ships	c
Australians	4	4	0	41	21	10.25	–	–	–	1
N.Zealanders	1	1	0	0	0	00.00	–	–	–	–
South Africans	3	3	0	68	54	22.66	–	1	–	2
Australian Imperial Forces	1	2	0	12	8	6.00	–	–	–	2
Cambridge University	10	16	1	403	77	26.86	–	3	1	4
England XI	1	1	0	74	74	74.00	–	1	1	2
Lancashire	2	3	0	34	26	11.33	–	–	–	–
MCC	14	22	4	680	120	37.77	2	3	3	10
Rest of England	6	10	2	195	63*	24.37	–	2	1	3
Totals	42	62	7	1507	120	27.40	2	10	6	24

BOWLING

Opponents	Overs	Mdns	Runs	Wkts	Avge	5 wkts in Inns	10 wkts in Match	Best in Inns
Australians	67	14	159	4	39.75	–	–	2:50
N. Zealanders	22	10	29	0	–	–	–	–
South Africans	86.3	37	139	12	11.58	–	–	4:30
Australian Imperial Forces	19	6	38	1	38.00	–	–	1:34
Cambridge University	238.2	70	528	22	24.00	–	–	4:71
England XI		Did	Not Bowl					
Lancashire	16.4	2	53	4	13.25	–	–	3:8
MCC	298.5	99	651	24	27.12	–	–	4:59
Rest of England	127	20	416	6	69.33	–	–	4:146
Totals	875.2	258	2013	73	27.57	–	–	4:30

TEST MATCHES

BATTING AND FIELDING

Opponents	M	I	No	Runs	HS	Avge	100s	50s	Cent. P'Ships	c
England v Australia	7	7	1	174	74	29.00	–	1	1	5
South Africa	2	1	–	59	59	59.00	–	1	–	1
Totals	9	8	1	233	74	33.28	–	2	1	6

BOWLING

Opponents	Overs	Mdns	Runs	Wkts	Avge	5 wkts in Inns	10 wkts in Match	Best in Inns
England v Australia	†179.1 121.5	66	675	24	28.12	–	–	4:51
South Africa	34	16	59	0	–	–	–	–
Totals	†179.1 155.5	82	734	24	30.58	–	–	4:51

† 8-ball overs

OTHER MATCHES – IN U.K.

BATTING AND FIELDING

Opponents	M	I	No	Runs	HS	Avge	100s	50s	Cent. P'Ships	c
England XI v Australians	1	1	1	12	12*	–	–	–	–	–
England XI v The Rest	3	5	1	94	37	23.50	–	–	–	2
MCC v CI Thornton's XI	1	1	0	7	7	7.00	–	–	–	–
North v South	2	4	1	93	31*	31.00	–	–	–	2
Players v Gentlemen	7	8	0	295	113	36.87	1	2	–	3
Rest of England v Royal Air Force	1	2	0	7	5	3.50	–	–	–	–
CI Thornton's XI v MCC	2	3	0	76	45	25.33	–	–	–	–
Uncapped v Capped	1	1	0	16	16	16.00	–	–	–	1
Totals	18	25	3	600	113	27.27	1	2	–	8

OTHER MATCHES – IN U.K.

BOWLING

Opponents	Overs	Mdns	Runs	Wkts	Avge	5 wkts in Inns	10 wkts in Match	Best in Inns
England XI v Australians	18	4	47	0	–	–	–	–
England XI v The Rest	121.4	47	209	10	20.90	–	–	3:49
MCC v CI Thornton's XI	22	9	49	3	16.33	–	–	2:17
North v South	51	15	126	13	9.69	1	–	5:11
Players v Gentlemen	211.5	63	496	18	27.55	1	–	6:20
Rest of England v Royal Air Force	29.3	7	69	4	17.25	–	–	3:55
CI Thornton's XI v MCC	29	12	61	3	20.33	–	–	3:44
Uncapped v Capped	26	7	64	2	32.00	–	–	2:43
Totals	509	164	1121	53	21.15	2	–	6:20

OTHER MATCHES – IN AUSTRALIA

BATTING AND FIELDING

Opponents	M	I	No	Runs	HS	Avge	100s	50s	Cent. P'Ships	c
MCC v Australian XI	1	1	0	52	52	52.00	–	1	–	–
New South Wales	2	4	0	31	19	7.75	–	–	–	2
South Australia	1	2	0	20	11	10.00	–	–	–	–
Tasmania	2	3	1	84	39	42.00	–	–	–	–
Victoria	2	3	0	29	20	9.66	–	–	–	1
Western Australia	1	1	0	103	103	103.00	1	–	1	–
Totals	9	14	1	319	103	24.53	1	1	1	3

BOWLING

Opponents	Overs	Mdns	Runs	Wkts	Avge	5 wkts in Inns	10 wkts in Match	Best in Inns
MCC v Australian XI	23	2	86	0	–	–	–	–
New South Wales	61.6	5	208	6	34.66	1	–	6:145
South Australia	5	0	24	0	–	–	–	–
Tasmania	31	5	105	6	17.50	1	–	5:35
Victoria	64.2	13	155	11	14.09	2	1	5:18
Western Australia	11	1	30	0	–	–	–	–
Totals	†196	26	608	23	26.43	4	1	6:145

† 8-ball overs

OTHER MATCHES – IN WEST INDIES

BATTING AND FIELDING

Opponents	M	I	No	Runs	HS	Avge	100s	50s	Cent. P'Ships	c
MCC v Barbados	2	4	0	81	45	20.25	–	–	–	3
British Guiana	2	2	1	31	19	31.00	–	–	–	1
Jamaica	3	3	2	65	54	65.00	–	1	–	5
Trinidad	2	2	0	15	9	7.50	–	–	–	2
West Indians	3	4	1	57	32	19.00	–	–	–	6
Totals	12	15	4	249	54	22.63	–	1	–	17

BOWLING

Opponents	Overs	Mdns	Runs	Wkts	Avge	5 wkts in Inns	10 wkts in Match	Best in Inns
MCC v Barbados	64	25	96	1	96.00	–	–	1:29
British Guiana	55.2	19	136	5	27.20	–	–	4:72
Jamaica	143.4	47	360	13	27.69	1	–	7:50
Trinidad	51	10	157	6	26.16	1	–	6:83
West Indians	110.5	27	254	9	28.22	–	–	3:60
Totals	424.5	128	1003	34	29.50	2	–	7:50

SUMMARY

BATTING AND FIELDING

	M	I	No	Runs	HS	Avge	100s	50s	Cent. P'Ships	c
County Championship	323	416	39	11511	206*	30.53	13	65	42	207
Other matches for Yorkshire	42	62	7	1507	120	27.40	2	10	6	24
Test Matches	9	8	1	233	74	33.28	–	2	1	6
Other matches in UK	18	25	3	600	113	27.27	1	2	–	8
Other matches in Australia	9	14	1	319	103	24.53	1	1	1	3
Other matches in West Indies	12	15	4	249	54	22.63	–	1	–	17
Totals	413	540	55	14419	206*	29.72	17	81	50	265

SUMMARY

BOWLING

	Overs	Mdns	Runs	Wkts	Avge	5 wkts in Inns	10 wkts in Match	Best in Inns
County Championship	7223.4	2702	12841	784	16.37	39	9	8:26
Other matches for Yorkshire	875.2	258	2013	73	27.57	–	–	4:30
Test matches	†179.1 155.5	82	734	24	30.58	–	–	4:51
Other matches in UK	509	164	1121	53	21.15	2	–	6:20
Other matches in Australia	†196	26	608	23	26.43	4	1	6:145
Other matches in West Indies	424.5	128	1003	34	29.50	2	–	7:50
Totals	†375.1 9188.4	3360	18320	991	18.48	47	10	8:26

† 8–ball overs

GROUNDS IN YORKSHIRE

BATTING AND FIELDING

Grounds	M	I	No	Runs	HS	Avge	100s	50s	Cent. P'Ships	c
Bradford	37	44	1	971	85	22.58	–	5	4	26
Dewsbury	12	16	0	472	124	29.50	1	1	2	9
Harrogate	14	15	0	721	150	48.06	1	5	3	10
Huddersfield	10	13	2	341	79	31.00	–	4	1	4
Hull	16	19	2	395	55	23.23	–	2	1	11
Leeds	37	51	4	1409	124	29.97	3	6	7	23
Scarborough	17	26	4	647	100*	29.40	1	3	1	8
Sheffield	44	58	4	1676	206*	31.03	1	10	5	22
Totals	187	242	17	6632	206*	29.47	7	36	24	113

BOWLING

Grounds	Overs	Mdns	Runs	Wkts	Avge	5 wkts in Inns	10 wkts in Match	Best in Inns
Bradford	832.1	328	1390	105	13.23	4	1	8:40
Dewsbury	277	98	552	29	19.03	1	–	5:35
Harrogate	223.1	91	380	34	11.17	2	1	6:22
Huddersfield	150.5	49	286	6	47.66	–	–	3:72
Hull	369	132	621	44	14.11	2	–	5:56
Leeds	820.4	309	1467	78	18.80	2	–	5:38
Scarborough	373.5	126	810	27	30.00	–	–	4:59
Sheffield	958.5	352	1833	88	20.82	4	1	6:22
Totals	4005.3	1485	7339	411	17.85	15	3	8:40

OTHER GROUNDS IN U.K. BATTING AND FIELDING

Grounds	M	I	No	Runs	HS	Avge	100s	50s	Cent. P'Ships	c
Bath	1		Did	Not	Bat					
Birmingham	13	19	5	700	121	50.00	1	6	1	11
Blackheath	1	1	0	59	59	59.00	–	1	–	–
Blackpool	1	1	1	12	12*	–	–	–	–	–
Bourne'mth	2	3	0	41	29	13.66	–	–	–	5
Bristol (County Ground)	4	6	0	222	169	37.00	1	–	1	1
Bristol (Greenbank)	2	3	0	12	7	4.00	–	–	–	2
Cambridge	10	16	1	403	77	26.86	–	3	1	4
Cardiff	5	4	1	108	42*	36.00	–	–	–	2
Chesterfield	6	5	0	178	62	35.60	–	1	1	3
Derby	3	4	1	209	90	69.66	–	2	2	5
Dover	1	1	0	0	0	00.00	–	–	–	1
Dudley	1	1	0	117	117	117.00	1	–	1	1
Eastbourne	2	4	1	66	31*	22.00	–	–	–	–
Gloucester (Spa Ground)	3	4	0	158	112	39.50	1	–	1	2
Gloucester (Wagon Wks Ground)	2	2	1	90	90*	90.00	–	1	–	–
Hastings	2	2	0	18	16	9.00	–	–	–	1
Hove	10	14	2	586	91*	48.83	–	6	2	3
Ilkeston	1	2	0	34	22	17.00	–	–	–	1
Kettering	1	1	1	2	2*	–	–	–	–	1
Leicester	11	14	1	257	49	19.76	–	–	–	4
Leyton	9	7	0	57	33	8.14	–	–	–	10
Liverpool	1	2	0	8	8	4.00	–	–	–	–
Lord's	21	29	4	1136	150	45.44	3	7	4	16
Maidstone	4	7	0	133	79	19.00	–	1	1	1
Manchester	15	22	2	322	50	16.10	–	1	–	14
N'thampton	10	13	2	471	166	42.81	1	3	2	12
Nottingham	13	17	2	541	137	36.06	1	3	4	10
The Oval	17	22	2	463	89	23.15	–	3	2	11
Portsmouth	4	3	1	86	77	43.00	–	1	–	1
S'hampton	5	6	0	130	51	21.66	–	1	–	3
Southend -on-Sea	1	1	0	10	10	10.00	–	–	–	–
Swansea	1	2	0	56	52	28.00	–	1	–	–
Taunton	5	7	2	80	43*	16.00	–	–	–	1
Tonbridge	2	3	0	119	79	39.66	–	1	1	–
Tunbridge Wells	3	4	0	87	30	21.75	–	–	–	1
Weston-super-Mare	1	2	0	6	4	3.00	–	–	–	–
Worcester	8	10	3	113	41	16.14	–	–	–	3
Totals	202	264	33	7090	169	30.69	9	42	24	130

BOWLING

Grounds	Overs	Mdns	Runs	Wkts	Avge	5 wkts in Inns	10 wkts in Match	Best in Inns
Bath	20	8	34	2	17.00	–	–	2:34
Birmingham	307.1	129	556	39	14.25	3	–	6:26
Blackheath	20	2	47	0	–	–	–	–
Blackpool	18	4	47	0	–	–	–	–
Bournemouth	62.5	20	98	10	9.80	1	1	6:13
Bristol (County Ground)	83	39	113	7	16.14	–	–	3:26
Bristol (Greenbank)	72	33	107	9	11.88	–	–	4:10
Cambridge	238.2	70	528	22	24.00	–	–	4:71
Cardiff	94.1	46	112	26	4.30	2	1	8:26
Chesterfield	86	30	158	11	14.36	–	–	4:24
Derby	82.5	31	123	14	8.78	1	–	5:32
Dover	10.3	5	10	2	5.00	–	–	1:4
Dudley	30	12	40	4	10.00	–	–	3:34
Eastbourne	53	16	113	12	9.41	1	–	5:11
Gloucester (Spa Ground)	12	3	32	1	32.00	–	–	1:32
Gloucester (Wagon Wks Ground)	93	29	153	10	15.30	–	–	4:21
Hastings	26	7	64	2	32.00	–	–	2:43
Hove	245	90	447	37	12.08	3	1	7:37
Ilkeston	24	11	25	4	6.25	–	–	4:25
Kettering	29	17	35	5	7.00	–	–	4:21
Leicester	327.2	145	475	24	19.79	1	–	5:84
Leyton	196.1	68	360	17	21.17	1	1	6:43
Liverpool	16.4	2	53	4	13.25	–	–	3:8
Lord's	660	197	1477	60	24.61	1	–	6:20
Maidstone	127.2	30	295	12	24.58	1	–	5:48
Manchester	394	162	612	28	21.85	1	–	5:33
Northampton	98.4	47	126	17	7.41	1	–	5:34
Nottingham	337.3	118	632	37	17.08	3	–	6:42
The Oval	436.2	122	1029	33	31.18	3	1	5:58
Portsmouth	126.3	48	219	21	10.42	2	1	6:15
Southampton	70	23	141	3	47.00	–	–	2:38
Southend-on-Sea	39	15	79	3	26.33	–	–	2:31
Swansea	42	12	110	2	55.00	–	–	2:110
Taunton	115.2	42	194	11	17.63	–	–	4:40
Tonbridge	31	4	78	1	78.00	–	–	1:34
Tunbridge Wells	16	3	47	0	–	–	–	–
Weston-super-Mare		Did	Not Bowl					
Worcester	117.4	46	202	16	12.62	1	–	5:74
Totals	4758.2	1686	8971	506	17.72	26	6	8:26

IN AUSTRALIA

BATTING AND FIELDING

Grounds	M	I	No	Runs	HS	Avge	100s	50s	Cent. P'Ships	c
Adelaide	2	4	0	50	24	12.50	–	–	–	1
Brisbane	1	1	0	52	52	52.00	–	1	–	–
Hobart	1	1	1	24	24*	–	–	–	–	–
Launceston	1	2	0	60	39	30.00	–	–	–	–
Melbourne	3	4	0	103	74	25 75	–	1	1	2
Perth	1	1	0	103	103	103.00	1	–	1	–
Sydney	3	6	0	56	24	9.33	–	–	–	2
Totals	12	19	1	448	103	24.88	1	2	2	5

BOWLING

Grounds	Overs	Mdns	Runs	Wkts	Avge	5 wkts in Inns	10 wkts in Match	Best in Inns
Adelaide	83.1	14	202	8	25.25	–	–	4:51
Brisbane	23	2	86	0	–	–	–	–
Hobart	14	3	33	1	33.00	–	–	1:22
Launceston	17	2	72	5	14.40	1	–	5:35
Melbourne	93.2	17	225	16	14.06	2	1	5:18
Perth	11	1	30	0	–	–	–	–
Sydney	133.6	22	359	10	35.90	1	–	6:145
Totals	†375.1	61	1007	40	25.17	4	1	6:145

† 8–ball overs

IN WEST INDIES

BATTING AND FIELDING

Grounds	M	I	No	Runs	HS	Avge	100s	50s	Cent. P'Ships	c
Barbados	3	5	0	81	45	16.20	–	–	–	7
Georgetown	3	4	2	56	19	28.00	–	–	–	1
Kingston (Melbourne Park)	1	1	0	54	54	54.00	–	1	–	2
Kingston (Sabina Park)	2	2	2	11	9*	–	–	–	–	3
Port-of-Spain	3	3	0	47	32	15.66	–	–	–	4
Totals	12	15	4	249	54	22.63	–	1	–	17

BOWLING

Grounds	Overs	Mdns	Runs	Wkts	Avge	5 wkts in Inns	10 wkts in Match	Best in Inns
Barbados	89	36	147	4	36.75	–	–	2:43
Georgetown	97.1	28	225	8	28.12	–	–	4:72
Kingston (Melbourne Park)	53	17	122	4	30.50	–	–	4:79
Kingston (Sabina Park)	90.4	30	238	9	26.44	1	–	7:50
Port-of-Spain	95	17	271	9	30.11	1	–	6:83
Totals	424.5	128	1003	34	29.50	2	–	7:50

SUMMARY

BATTING AND FIELDING

Grounds	M	I	No	Runs	HS	Avge	100s	50s	Cent. P'Ships	c
In Yorkshire	187	242	17	6632	206*	29.47	7	36	24	113
Others in UK	202	264	33	7090	169	30.69	9	42	24	130
In Australia	12	19	1	448	103	24.88	1	2	2	5
In West Indies	12	15	4	249	54	22.63	–	1	–	17
Totals	413	540	55	14419	206*	29.72	17	81	50	265

BOWLING

Grounds	Overs	Mdns	Runs	Wkts	Avge	5 wkts in Inns	10 wkts in Match	Best in Inns
In Yorkshire	4005.3	1485	7339	411	17.85	15	3	8:40
Others in UK	4758.2	1686	8971	506	17.72	26	6	8:26
In Australia	†375.1	61	1007	40	25.17	4	1	6:145
In West Indies	424.5	128	1003	34	29.50	2	–	7:50
Totals	†375.1 9188.4	3360	18320	991	18.48	47	10	8:26

†8-ball overs

CENTURIES

206* Yorkshire v Derbyshire at Sheffield, 1920
169 Yorkshire v Gloucestershire at Bristol, 1914
166 Yorkshire v Northamptonshire at Northampton, 1921
150 Yorkshire v Northamptonshire at Harrogate, 1921
150 Yorkshire v Middlesex at Lord's, 1926
137 Yorkshire v Nottinghamshire at Nottingham, 1920
124 Yorkshire v Northamptonshire at Leeds, 1922
124 Yorkshire v Warwickshire at Dewsbury, 1925
121 Yorkshire v Warwickshire at Birmingham, 1920
120 Yorkshire v MCC at Lord's, 1919
117 Yorkshire v Worcestershire at Dudley, 1922
115* Yorkshire v Gloucestershire at Leeds, 1919
113 Players v Gentlemen at Lord's, 1924
112 Yorkshire v Gloucestershire at Gloucester, 1919
104 Yorkshire v Leicestershire at Leeds, 1913
103 MCC v Western Australia at Perth, 1924-25
100* Yorkshire v MCC at Scarborough, 1925

CENTURY PARTNERSHIPS EXCEEDING 150 RUNS

299 for 4th Wkt RK (150) and P. Holmes (277*) v Northamptonshire at Harrogate, 1921

276 for 5th Wkt RK (166) and W. Rhodes (104*) v Northamptonshire at Northampton, 1921

236 for 3rd Wkt RK (137) and H. Sutcliffe (107) v Nottinghamshire at Nottingham, 1920

205 for 4th Wkt RK (117) and E. Oldroyd (121) v Worcestershire at Dudley, 1922

196* for 5th Wkt RK (115*) and G.H. Hirst (82*) v Gloucestershire at Leeds, 1919

184 for 6th Wkt RK (104) and M.W. Booth (79) v Leicestershire at Leeds, 1913

177 for 3rd Wkt RK (88) and D.Denton (124) v Sussex at Hove, 1914

176 for 3rd Wkt RK (90) and E. Oldroyd (82) v Derbyshire at Derby, 1922

175 for 5th Wkt RK (77) and A. Drake (108) v Cambridge University at Cambridge, 1913

173 for 3rd Wkt RK (89) and H. Sutcliffe (232) v Surrey at The Oval, 1922

173 for 5th Wkt RK (124) and H. Sutcliffe (206) v Warwickshire at Dewsbury, 1925

170 for 5th Wkt RK (87) and W. Rhodes (157) v Derbyshire at Leeds, 1925

169 for 4th Wkt RK (120) and G.H. Hirst (180*) v MCC at Lord's, 1919
165 for 3rd Wkt RK (112) and W. Rhodes (72) v Gloucestershire at Gloucester, 1919
151* for 5th Wkt RK (50*) and GH. Hirst (102*) v Kent at Bradford, 1913
151 for 5th Wkt RK (90) and W. Rhodes (57) v Nottinghamshire at Nottingham, 1925

10 WICKETS IN A MATCH

12:55	(5:18 and 7:37)	Yorkshire v Sussex at Hove, 1924*
11:48	(5:33 and 6:15)	Yorkshire v Hampshire at Portsmouth, 1924*
11:51	(5:29 and 6:22)	Yorkshire v Essex at Harrogate, 1922
10:41	(2:15 and 8:26)	Yorkshire v Glamorgan at Cardiff, 1923
10:66	(5:48 and 5:18)	MCC v Victoria at Melbourne, 1924-25
10:90	(4:77 and 6:13)	Yorkshire v Hampshire at Bournemouth, 1922
10:100	(4:78 and 6:22)	Yorkshire v Surrey at Sheffield, 1923
10:116	(6:43 and 4:73)	Yorkshire v Essex at Leyton, 1926
10:117	(2:77 and 8:40)	Yorkshire v Middlesex at Bradford, 1926
10:153	(5:58 and 5:95)	Yorkshire v Surrey at The Oval, 1924*

* Consecutive Matches

CENTURY AND SIX WICKETS IN A MATCH

113 and 6:20 Players v Gentlemen at Lord's, 1924
124 and 4:108 and 2:44 Yorkshire v Warwickshire at Dewsbury, 1925

4 CATCHES IN A MATCH

5 Yorkshire v Northamptonshire at Northampton, 1924
5 Yorkshire v Essex at Leyton, 1926
4 Yorkshire v Somerset at Bradford, 1913
4 Yorkshire v Hampshire at Bournemouth, 1922
4 MCC v West Indians at Barbados, 1925-26

HOW OUT

c	279	57.52%
b	124	25.57%
lbw	47	9.70%
st	15	3.09%
Ro	17	3.50%
Hw	3	0.62%
	485	100.00%

HOW WICKETS TAKEN

c	512	51.67%
b	286	28.86%
lbw	133	13.42%
st	56	5.65%
Hw	4	0.40%
	991	100.00%

THE DOUBLE

Roy Kilner achieved the double of 1000 runs and 100 wickets in a season on 4 occasions (1922, 1923, 1925 and 1926). Wilfred Rhodes (16), George Hirst (14) and Raymond Illingworth (6) are the only Yorkshiremen to have performed the double more often.

INDEX